Piano · Vocal · Guitar

HOLLYWOOD
Love Songs

1930s to 1990s

W9-ANH-305

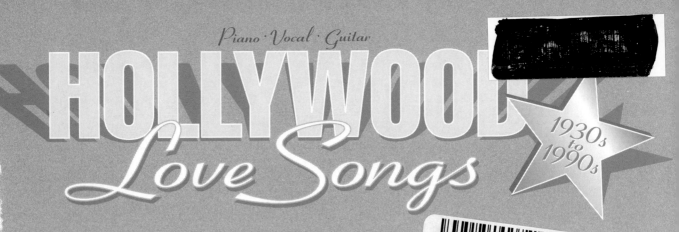

ISBN 0-7935-8345-4

HAL•LEONARD®
CORPORATION

7777 W. BLUEMOUND RD. P.O. BOX 13819 MILWAUKEE, WI 53213

Visit Hal Leonard Online at
www.halleonard.com

CONTENTS
Alphabetically by Song Title

CONTENTS
Chronologically by Decade

ALWAYS IN MY HEART
(Sienpre en mi Corazón)
from ALWAYS IN MY HEART

English Lyric by KIM GANNON
Original Words and Music by ERNESTO LECUONA

Moderately

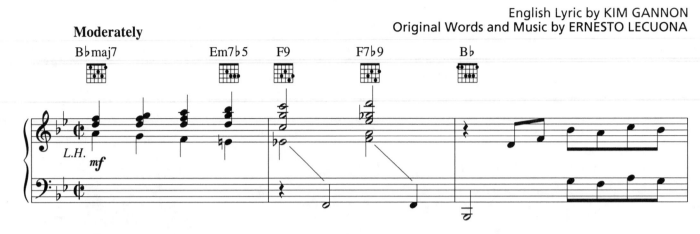

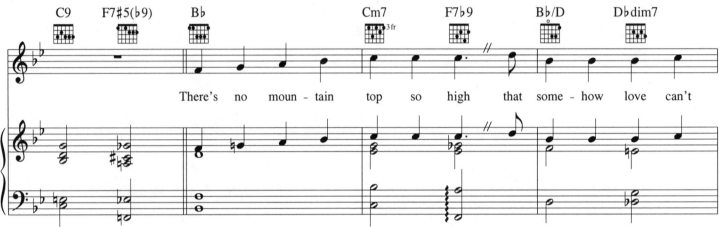

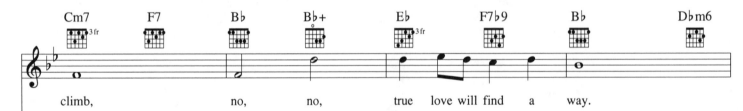

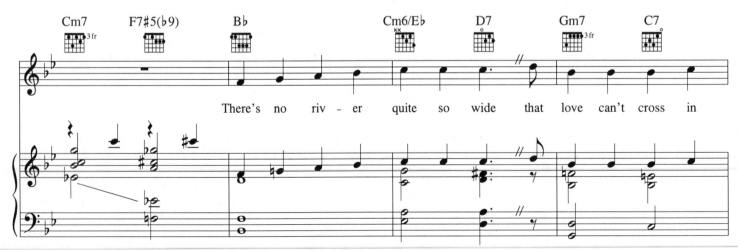

BEAUTY AND THE BEAST

from Walt Disney's BEAUTY AND THE BEAST

Lyrics by HOWARD ASHMAN
Music by ALAN MENKEN

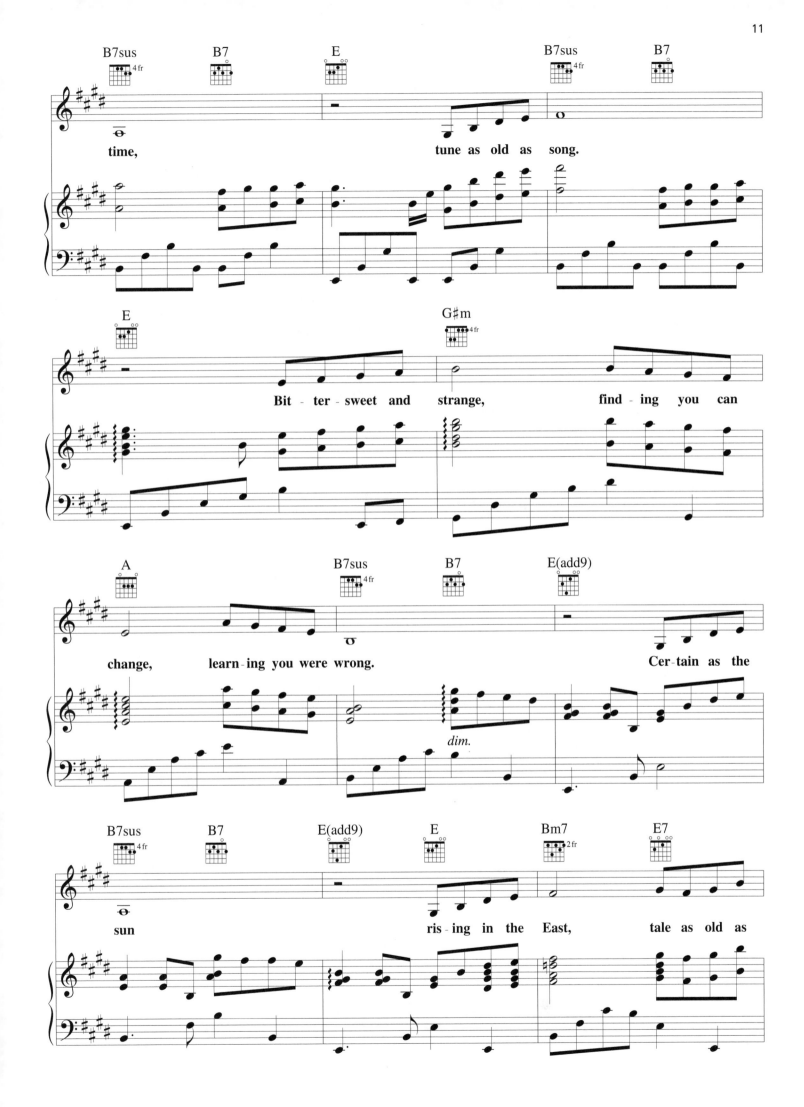

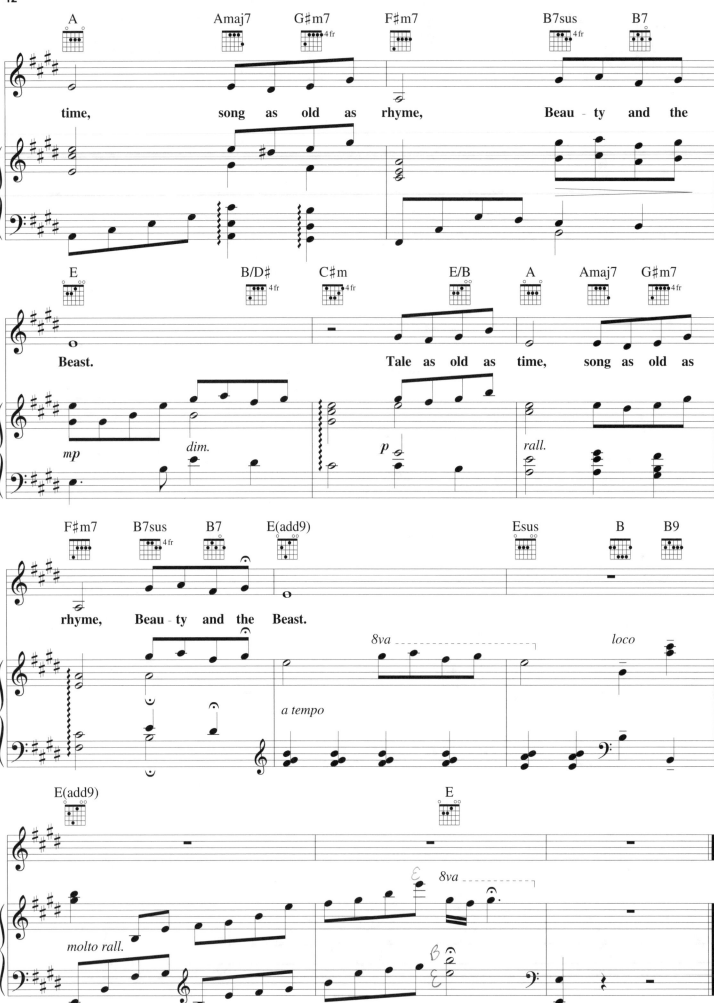

THE BEST THINGS HAPPEN WHILE YOU'RE DANCING

from the Motion Picture Irving Berlin's WHITE CHRISTMAS

Words and Music by
IRVING BERLIN

The best things _____ hap-pen while you're danc - ing. _____ Things that you would not do at home come nat-ur-'lly on the floor. _____ For

dance - ing _____ soon be-comes ro - manc - ing _____

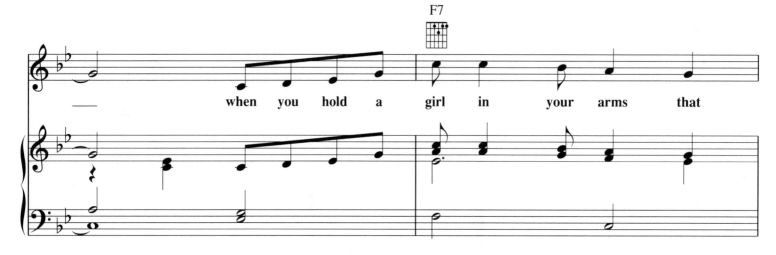

_____ when you hold a girl in your arms that

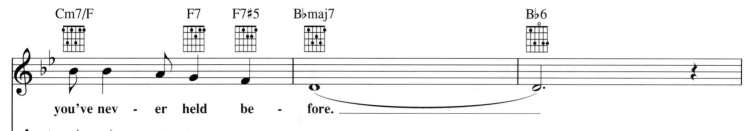

you've nev - er held be - fore. _____

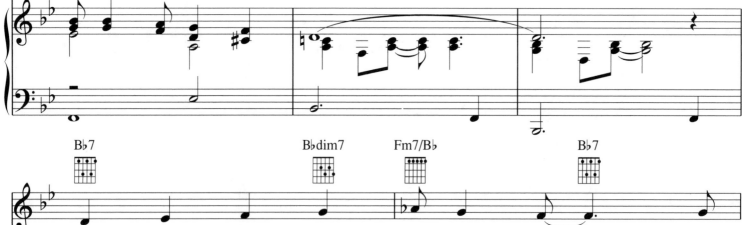

E - ven guys with two left feet _____ come

BETTER LUCK NEXT TIME

from the Motion Picture Irving Berlin's EASTER PARADE

Words and Music by
IRVING BERLIN

BLUE VELVET
featured in the Motion Picture BLUE VELVET

Words and Music by BERNIE WAYNE
and LEE MORRIS

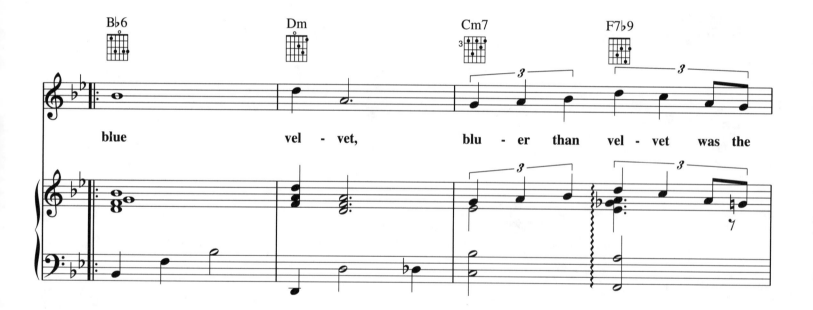

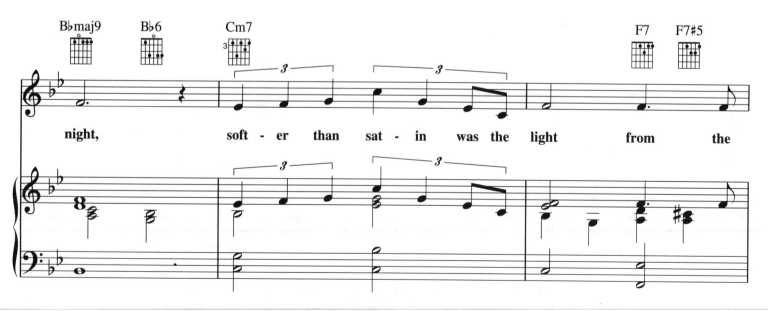

CA, C'EST L'AMOUR
from LES GIRLS

Words and Music by
COLE PORTER

Moderately

When sud-den-ly you sight some-one for whom you yearn, Ca,*)

C'est*) L'a - mour. And when to your de - light she

loves you in re - turn, Ca, C'est L'a - mour.

*pronounce: sah, say

CALL ME IRRESPONSIBLE

from the Paramount Picture PAPA'S DELICATE CONDITION

Words by SAMMY CAHN
Music by JAMES VAN HEUSEN

Do my fool- ish al- i- bis

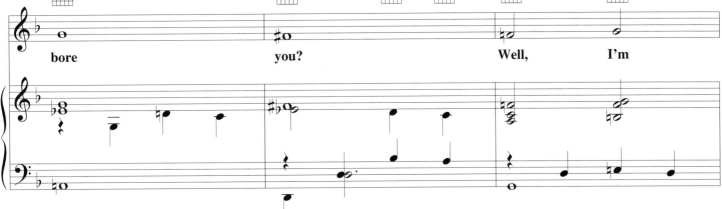

bore you? Well, I'm

not too clev- er. I just a-

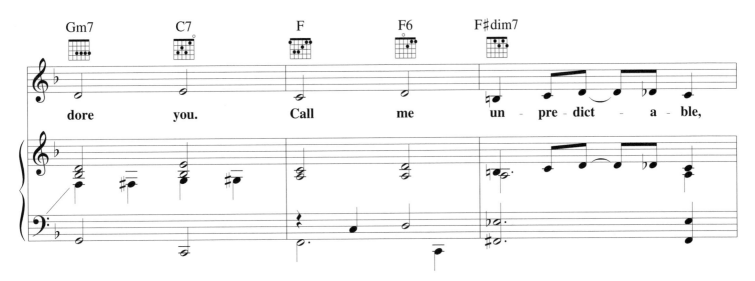

dore you. Call me un- pre- dict- a- ble,

tell me I'm im-prac-ti-cal, rain-bows I'm in-clined to pur-sue.

Call me ir-re-spon-si-ble,

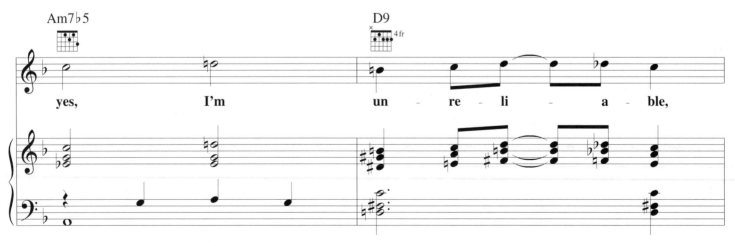

yes, I'm un-re-li-a-ble,

CAN YOU FEEL THE LOVE TONIGHT

from Walt Disney Pictures' THE LION KING

Music by ELTON JOHN
Lyrics by TIM RICE

kings ___ and ___ vag - a - bonds ___ be - lieve the ver - y best. ___

kings ___ and ___ vag-a-bonds ___ be-lieve the ver - y best. ___

It's e - nough ___ to make

CAN'T HELP FALLING IN LOVE

from BLUE HAWAII

Words and Music by GEORGE DAVID WEISS,
HUGO PERETTI and LUIGI CREATORE

CHANGE THE WORLD

featured on the Motion Picture Soundtrack PHENOMENON

Words and Music by GORDON KENNEDY,
TOMMY SIMS and WAYNE KIRKPATRICK

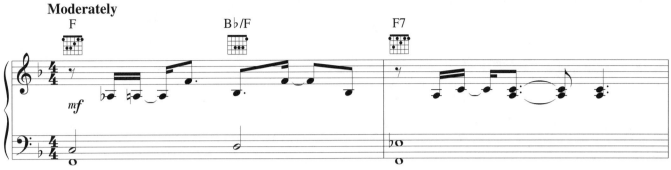

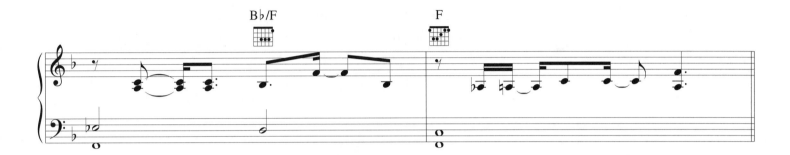

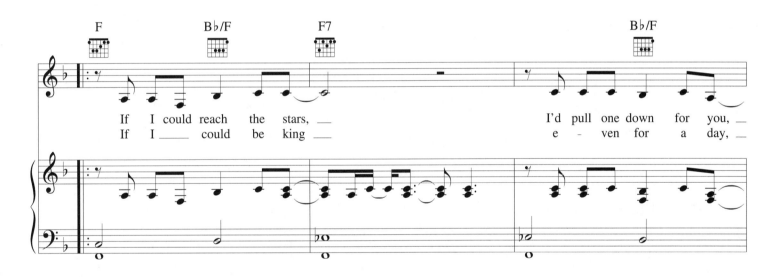

If I could reach the stars, ___   I'd pull one down for you, ___
If I ___ could be king ___   e - ven for a day, ___

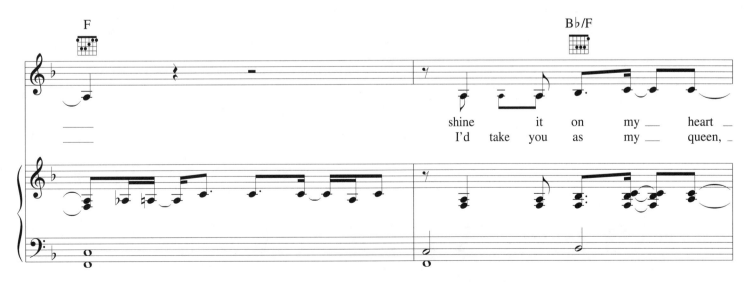

___ shine it on my ___ heart ___
___ I'd take you as my ___ queen, ___

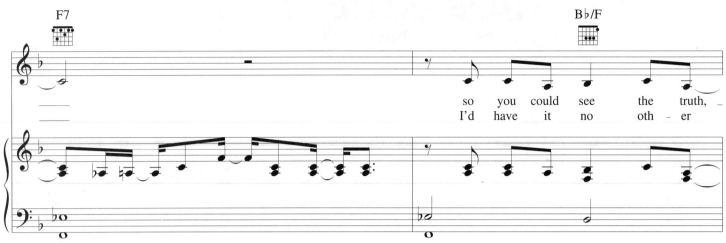

so you could see the truth, __
I'd have it no oth - er

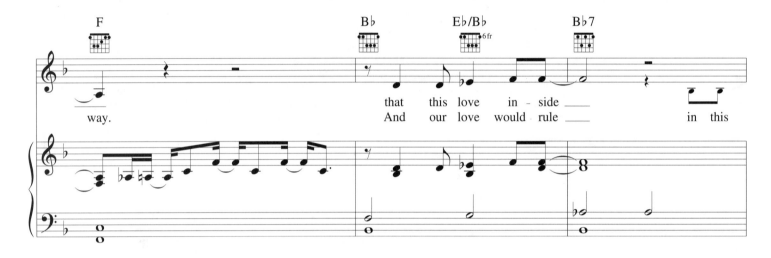

way.

that this love in - side ____
And our love would rule ____ in this

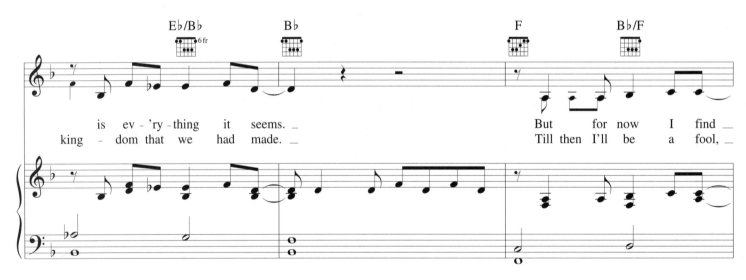

is ev - 'ry -thing it seems. _
king - dom that we had made. _

But for now I find _
Till then I'll be a fool, _

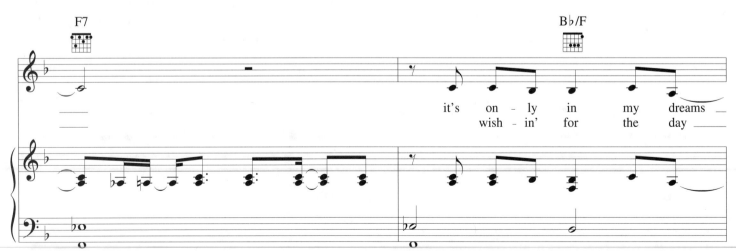

it's on - ly in my dreams _
wish - in' for the day ____

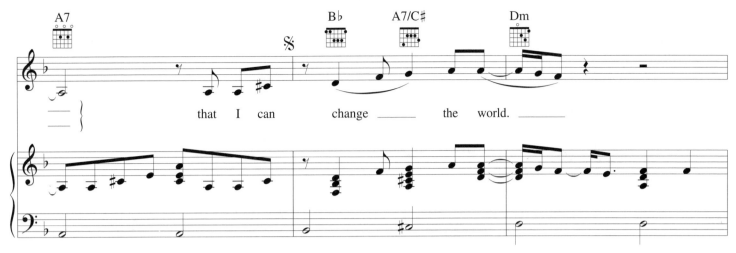

that I can change _____ the world. _____

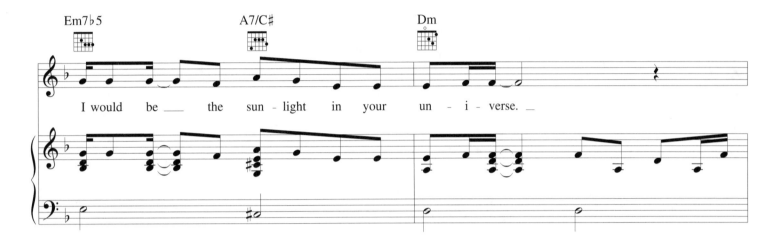

I would be ___ the sun-light in your un - i - verse. __

You would think _ my love was real - ly some -thin' good, _ ba - by,

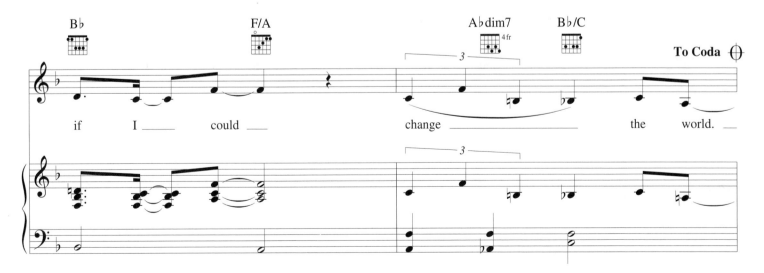

if I _____ could ___ change _____ the world. __

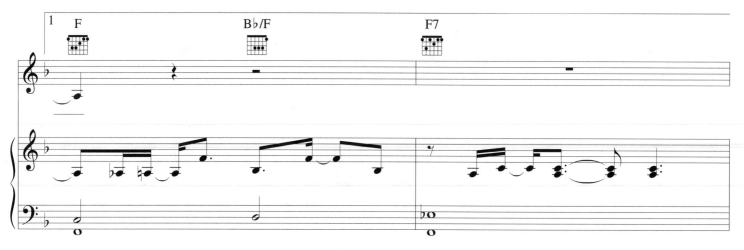

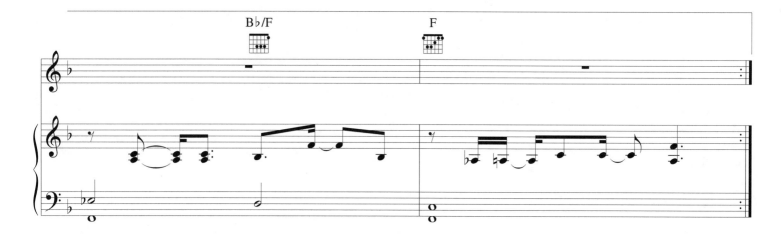

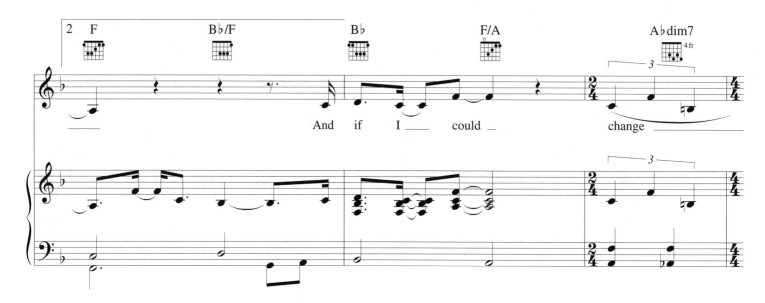

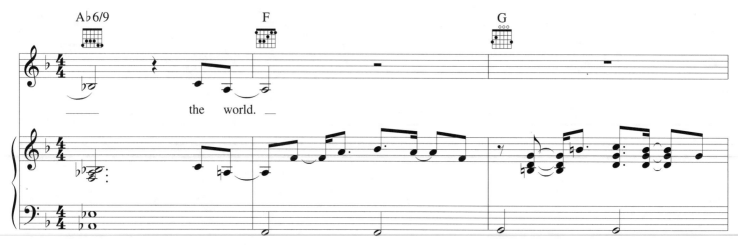

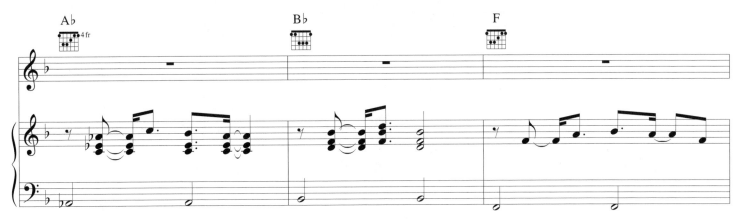

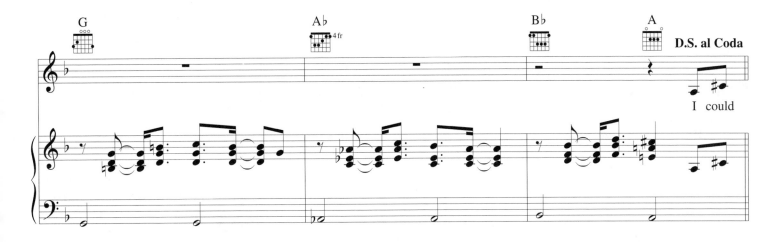

CHANGE PARTNERS
from the RKO Radio Motion Picture CAREFREE

Words and Music by
IRVING BERLIN

Must you dance _____ ev - 'ry dance _____ with the same _____ for - tu - nate man? _____ You have danced with him since the mu - sic be - gan. _____

CHEEK TO CHEEK
from the RKO Radio Motion Picture TOP HAT

Words and Music by
IRVING BERLIN

Heav - en, _____ I'm in Heav - en. _____

And my heart beats so that I can hard - ly speak. _____

COULD I HAVE THIS DANCE
from URBAN COWBOY

Words and Music by WAYLAND HOLYFIELD
and BOB HOUSE

Moderately Slow

I'll al-ways re-mem-ber the song they were play-ing the
al-ways re-mem-ber that mag-ic mo-ment, when

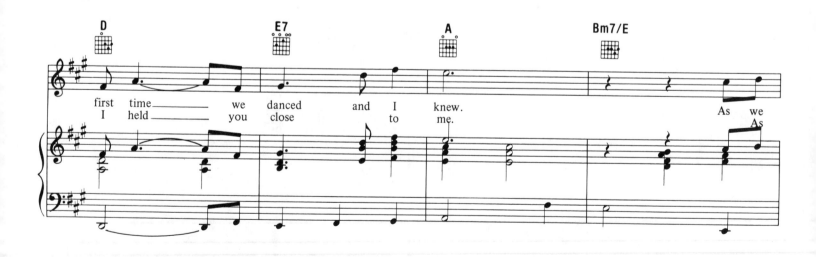

first time____ we danced and I knew.
I held____ you close to me.

As we
As

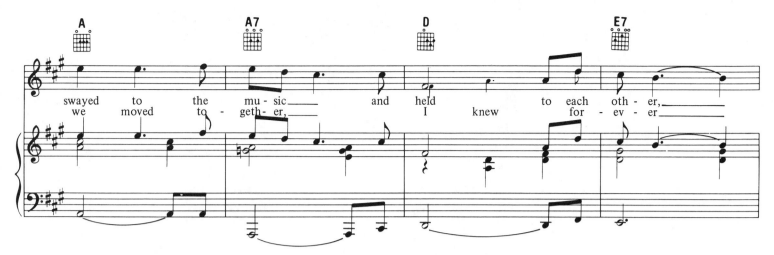

swayed to the mu - sic_____ and held to each oth - er,_____
we moved to - geth - er,_____ I knew for - ev - er_____

I fell in love _____ with _____ you.}
you're all I'll ev - er_____ need.}   Could

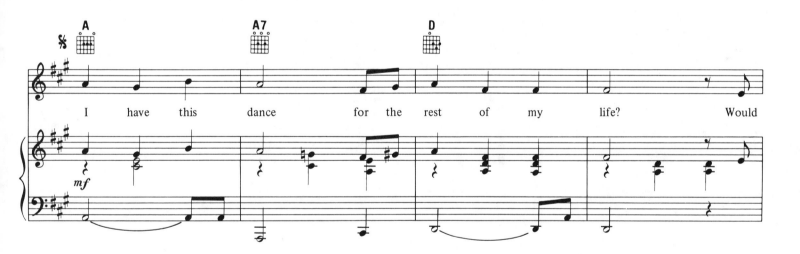

I have this dance for the rest of my life?   Would

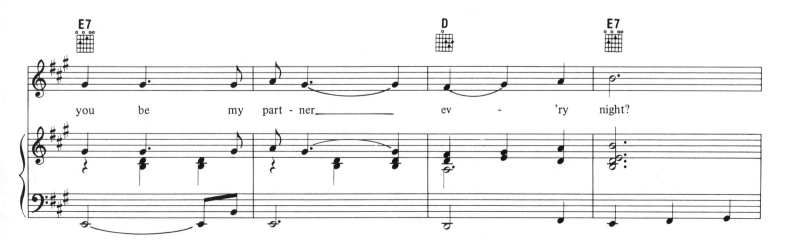

you be my part - ner_____ ev - 'ry night?

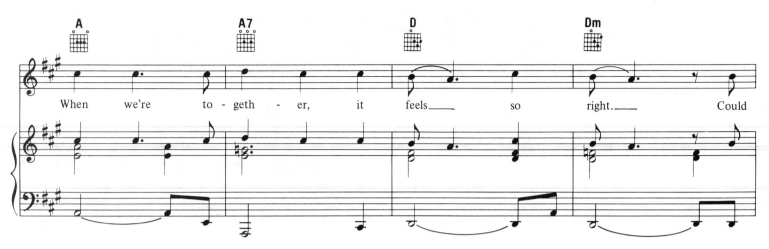

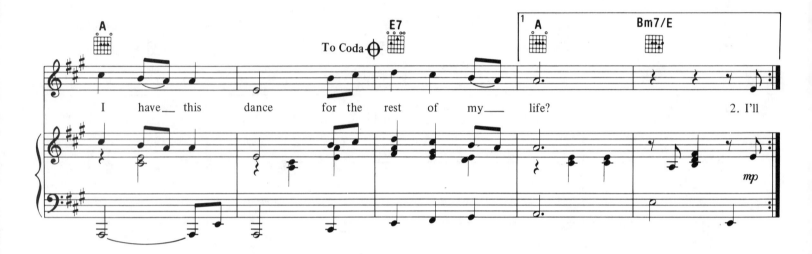

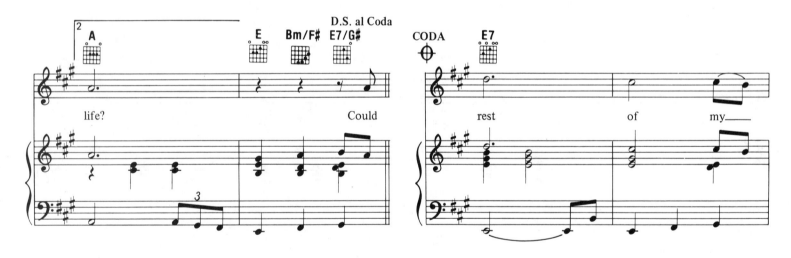

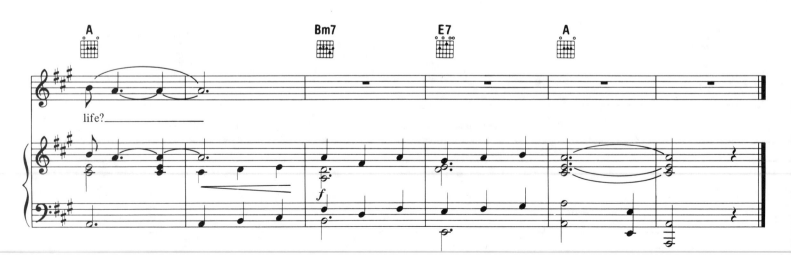

ENDLESS LOVE

from ENDLESS LOVE

Words and Music by
LIONEL RICHIE

EASY TO LOVE
(You'd Be So Easy to Love)
from BORN TO DANCE

Words and Music by
COLE PORTER

Moderately

mf espr.

You'd be so eas - y to love, So eas - y to i - dol - ize, all oth - ers a - bove, So worth the yearn - ing for,_____ So swell to keep ev' - ry home fire burn-

FOR ALL WE KNOW

from the Motion Picture LOVERS AND OTHER STRANGERS

Words by ROBB WILSON and JAMES GRIFFIN
Music by FRED KARLIN

Moderato, with a light beat

Love,_____ look at the two of us,_____ Stran-

gers _____ in man-y ways._____

MCA music publishing

GLORY OF LOVE
Theme from KARATE KID PART II

Words and Music by DAVID FOSTER,
PETER CETERA and DIANE NINI

Slowly

To-night__ it's ver-y clear, as we're both stand-ing here,__ there's__ so man-y things I want__ to say.__

I will al-ways love you, ___ I will nev-er leave you ___ a - lone. ___

Some-times I just for - get, say things I might re - gret, ___
You keep me stand-ing tall, you help me through it all, ___

it breaks my heart ___ to see ___ you cry - ing.
I'm al - ways strong ___ when you're ___ be - side me.

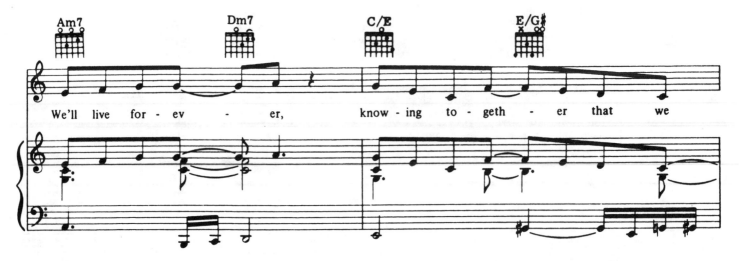

We'll live for - ev - er, know - ing to - geth - er that we

did it all for the glo - ry of love. _____

Just like a knight in shin-ing ar - mor, from a long time a-go,

just in time I will save the day, __ take you to my cas - tle far a - way. _____

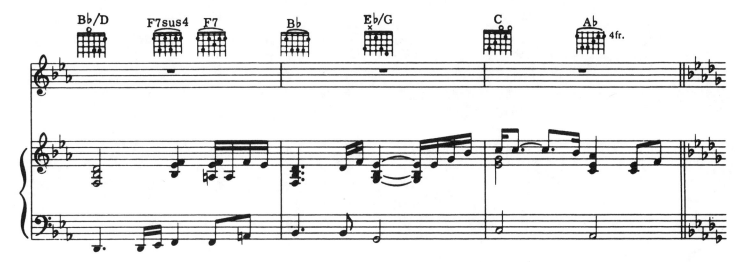

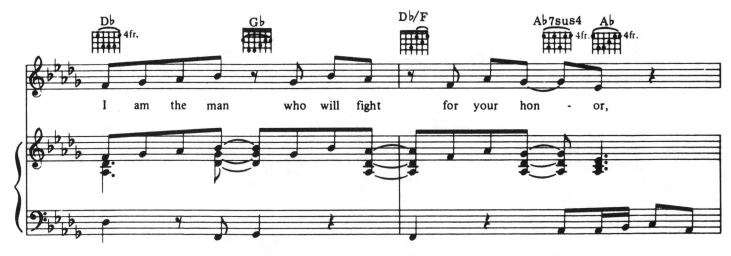

I am the man who will fight for your hon - or,

I'll be the he - ro that you're __ dream - ing of. __ We're

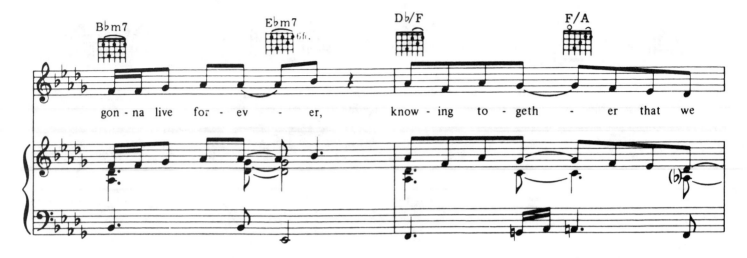

gon - na live for - ev - er, know-ing to-geth - er that we

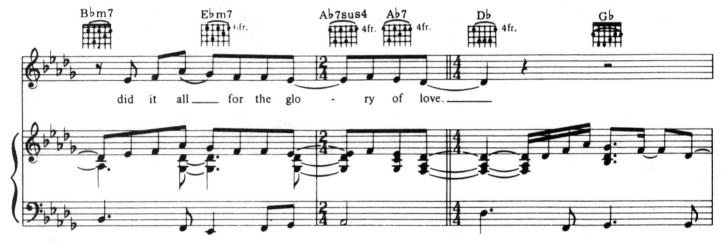

did it all ___ for the glo - ry of love. ___

We'll live for - ev - er, know-ing to-geth - er that we

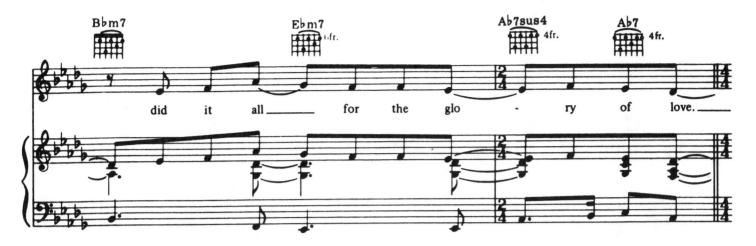

did it all _____ for the glo - ry of love. _____

We did __ it all __ for love. __

Repeat and fade

We did __ it all __ for love. __

We did __ it all __ for love. __

THE GLORY OF LOVE
from GUESS WHO'S COMING TO DINNER

Words and Music by
BILLY HILL

HOW DEEP IS YOUR LOVE
from the Motion Picture SATURDAY NIGHT FEVER

Words and Music by BARRY GIBB,
MAURICE GIBB and ROBIN GIBB

Moderately

I know your eyes in the morn - ing sun.____ I feel you touch
I be - lieve in you.____ You know the door

____ me in the pour - ing rain.____ And the mo - ment that you wan - der far
____ to my ver - y soul.____ You're the light ____ in my deep - est, dark

HOPELESSLY DEVOTED TO YOU

from GREASE

Words and Music by
JOHN FARRAR

Moderate 2

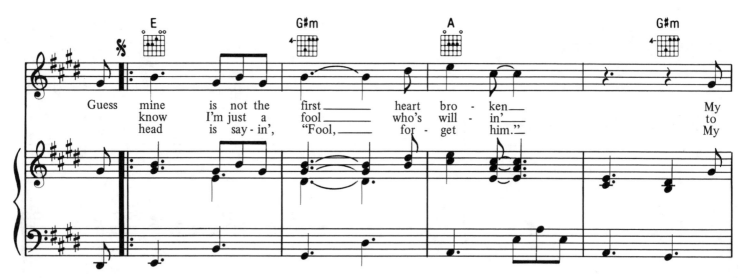

E   G#m   A   G#m

Guess mine is not the first ___ heart bro-ken ___ My
know I'm just a fool ___ who's will-in' ___ to
head is say-in', "Fool, ___ for-get him." My

F#m7   B7   E

eyes are not the first ___ to cry. I'm
sit a-round and wait ___ for you. But,
heart is say-in', "Don't ___ let go.

I CONCENTRATE ON YOU
from BROADWAY MELODY OF 1940

Words and Music by
COLE PORTER

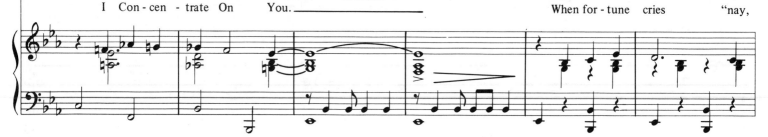

I FINALLY FOUND SOMEONE

from THE MIRROR HAS TWO FACES

Words and Music by BARBRA STREISAND, MARVIN HAMLISCH,
R. J. LANGE and BRYAN ADAMS

It's all you had to say __ to take my breath a - way. __

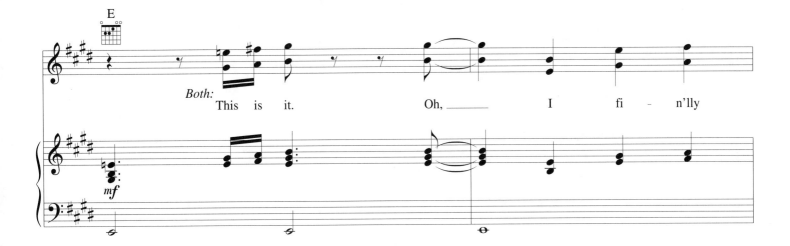

Both: This is it. Oh, ___ I fi - n'lly

found some - one, some - one to share __ my life. I fi - n'lly

found the one __ to be with ev - 'ry night. *Female:* 'Cause what -

ev - er I do, _____ *Male:* it's just got to be you. *Both:* My

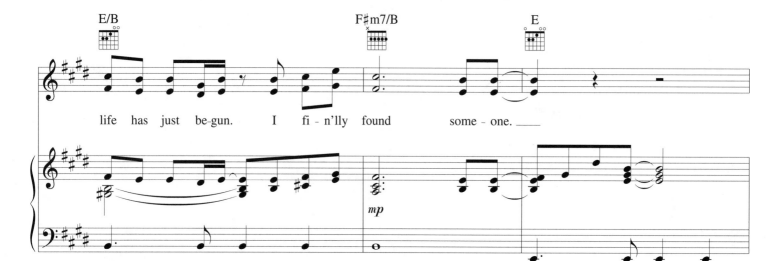

life has just be-gun. I fi - n'lly found some - one. _____

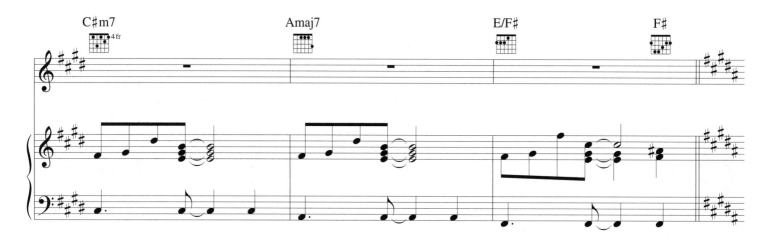

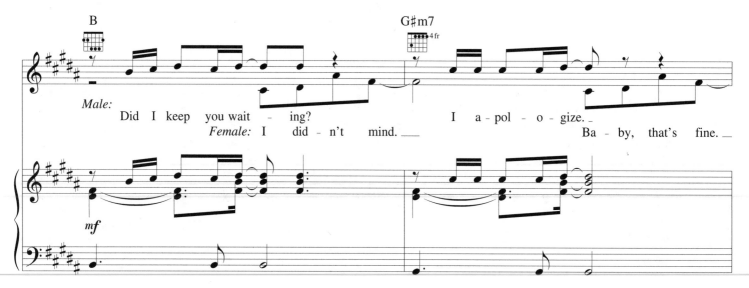

Male: Did I keep you wait - ing? I a - pol - o - gize. _

Female: I did - n't mind. ___ Ba - by, that's fine. _

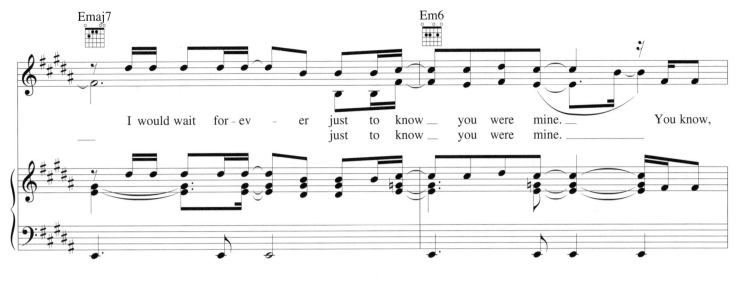

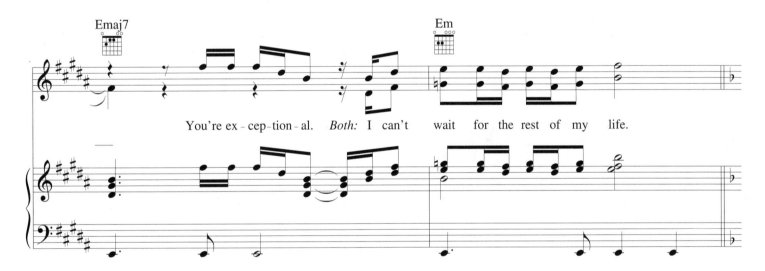

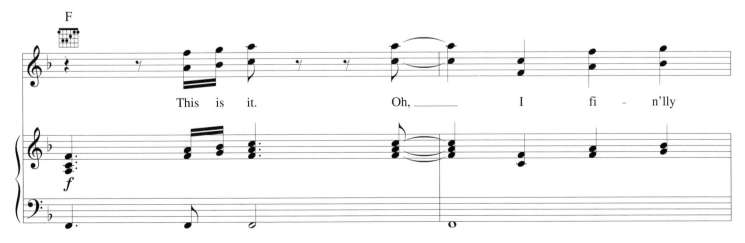

found some - one, some - one to share __ my life. I fi - n'lly

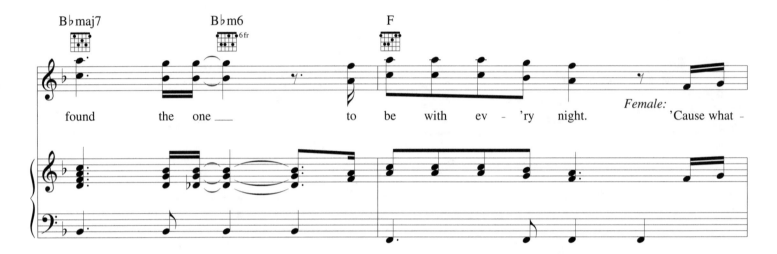

found the one __ to be with ev - 'ry night. *Female:* 'Cause what -

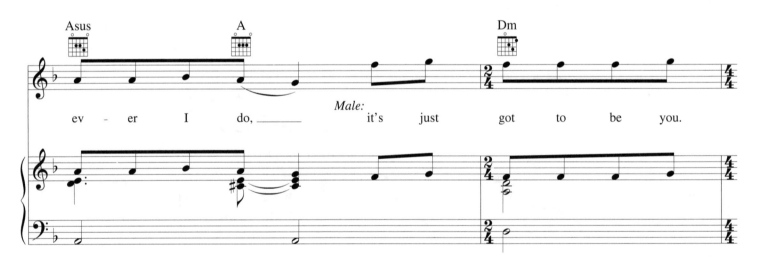

ev - er I do, _____ *Male:* it's just got to be you.

Both: My life has just __ be - gun. I fi - n'lly

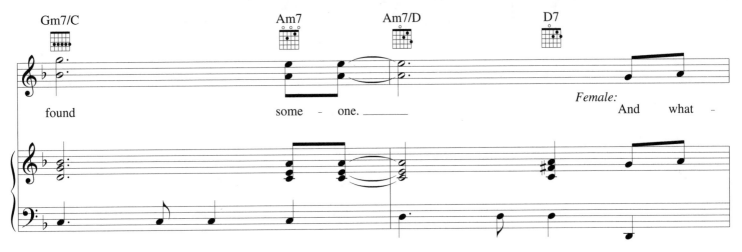

found   some - one. _____   *Female:* And   what -

ev - er   I   do, _____   *Male:* it's   just   got   to   be _____   you.   *Female:* My

life   has   just   be - gun. _____   *Both:* I   fi - n'lly

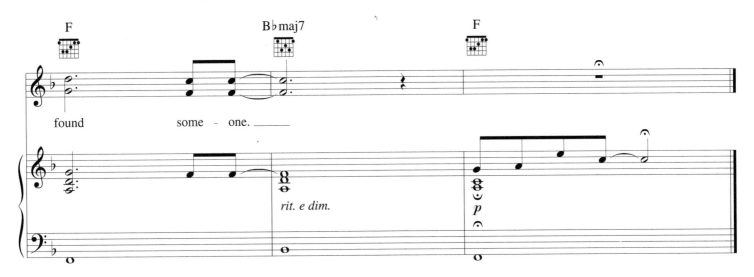

found   some - one. _____

I WILL WAIT FOR YOU

from THE UMBRELLAS OF CHERBOURG

Music by MICHEL LEGRAND
Original French Text by JACQUES DEMY
English Lyrics by NORMAN GIMBEL

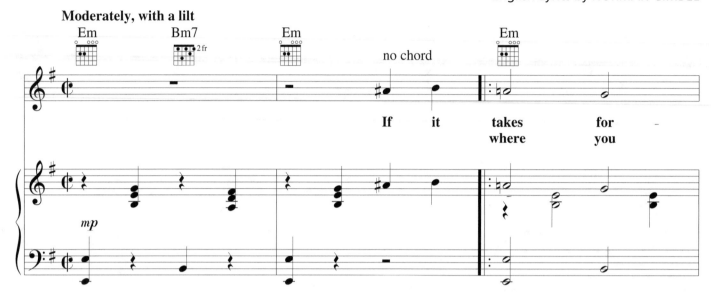

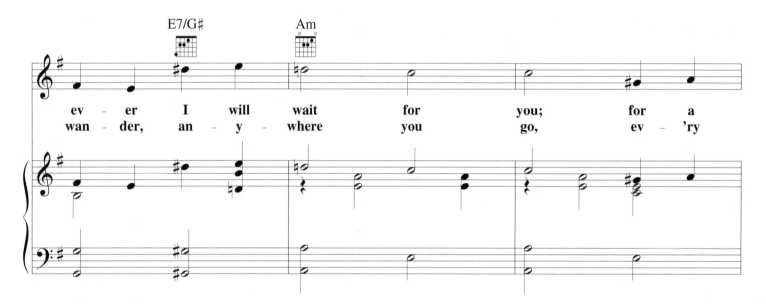

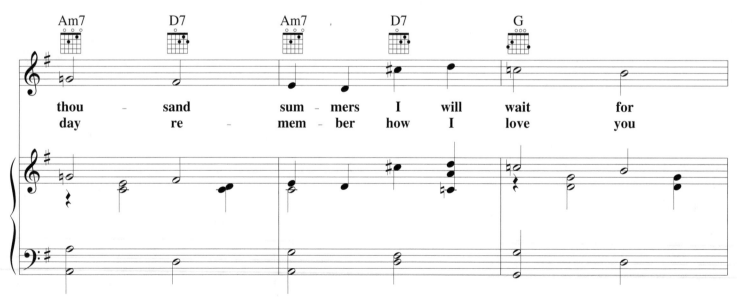

I WISH I DIDN'T LOVE YOU SO

from the Paramount Picture THE PERILS OF PAULINE

Words and Music by
FRANK LOESSER

I'VE GOT YOU UNDER MY SKIN

from BORN TO DANCE

Words and Music by
COLE PORTER

IF YOU REMEMBER ME

from THE CHAMP

Words by CAROLE BAYER SAGER
Music by MARVIN HAMLISCH

Moderately slow

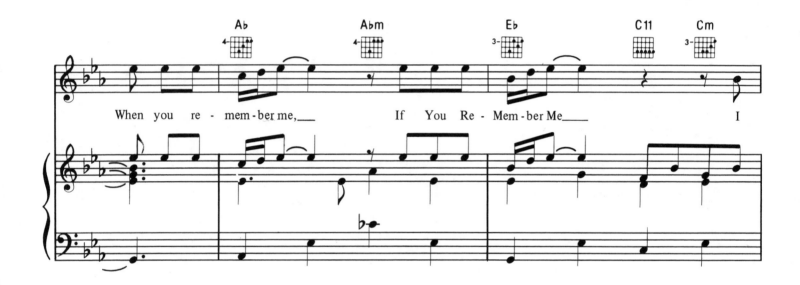

When you re-mem-ber me,___ If You Re-Mem-ber Me___ I

hope you see   it's not the way   I want it to be.___ Oh, I'd be with you now,___ but wher-

ISN'T IT ROMANTIC?
from the Paramount Picture LOVE ME TONIGHT

Words by LORENZ HART
Music by RICHARD RODGERS

Lyrics:

I've never met you, yet never doubt, dear,
I can't forget you, I've thought you out, dear.
I know your pro-file and I know the way you

My face is glow-ing, I'm ener-get-ic.
the art of sew-ing, I found po-et-ic.
My nee-dle punc-tu-ates the rhy-thm of ro-

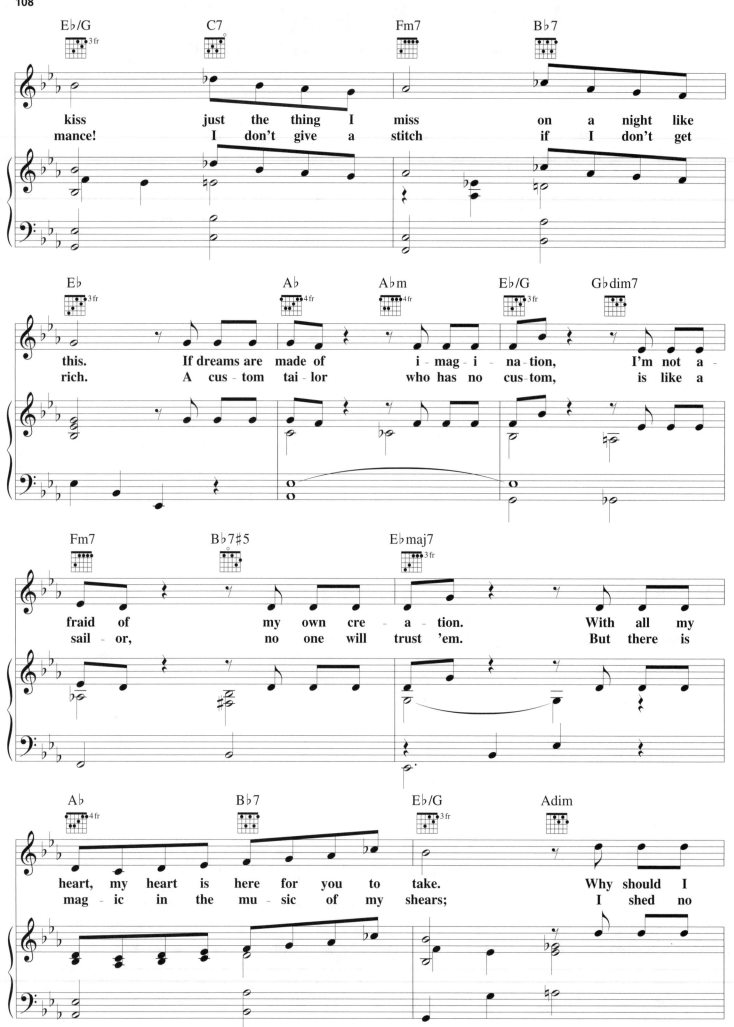

IN THE STILL OF THE NIGHT
from ROSALIE

Words and Music by
COLE PORTER

ISN'T THIS A LOVELY DAY
(To Be Caught in the Rain?)
from the RKO Radio Motion Picture TOP HAT

Words and Music by
IRVING BERLIN

The weath-er is fright-'ning, the thun-der and light-'ning seem to be hav-ing their way. But as far as I'm con-cerned, it's a love-ly day. _____ The

IT ONLY HAPPENS WHEN I DANCE WITH YOU

from the Motion Picture Irving Berlin's EASTER PARADE

Words and Music by
IRVING BERLIN

It on-ly hap-pens when I dance with you, ___

that trip to heav-en 'till the dance is through. ___

With no one else do the heav-ens seem

IT COULD HAPPEN TO YOU
from the Paramount Picture AND THE ANGELS SING

Words by JOHNNY BURKE
Music by JAMES VAN HEUSEN

IT'S A NEW WORLD
from the Motion Picture A STAR IS BORN

Lyric by IRA GERSHWIN
Music by HAROLD ARLEN

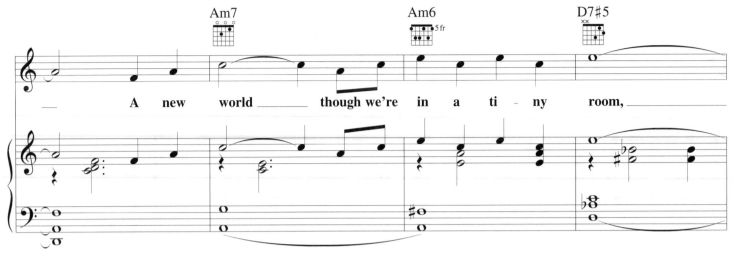

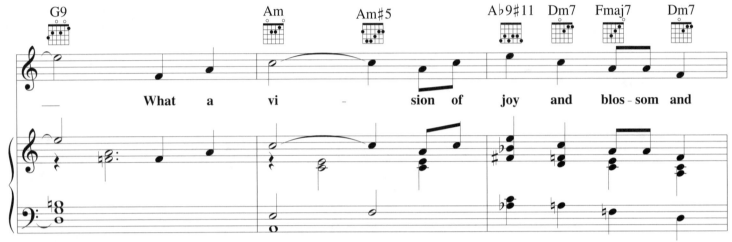

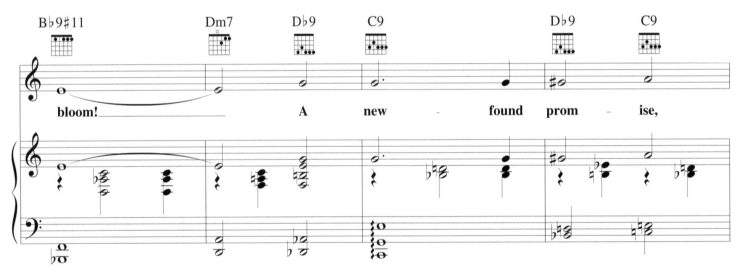

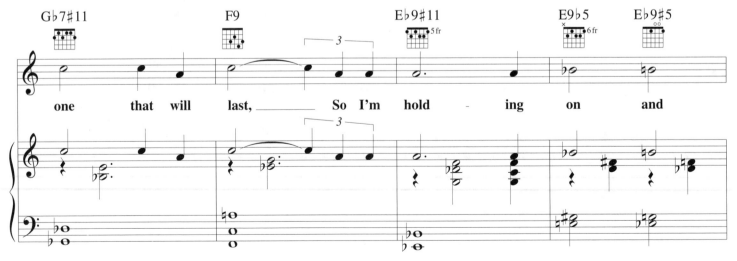

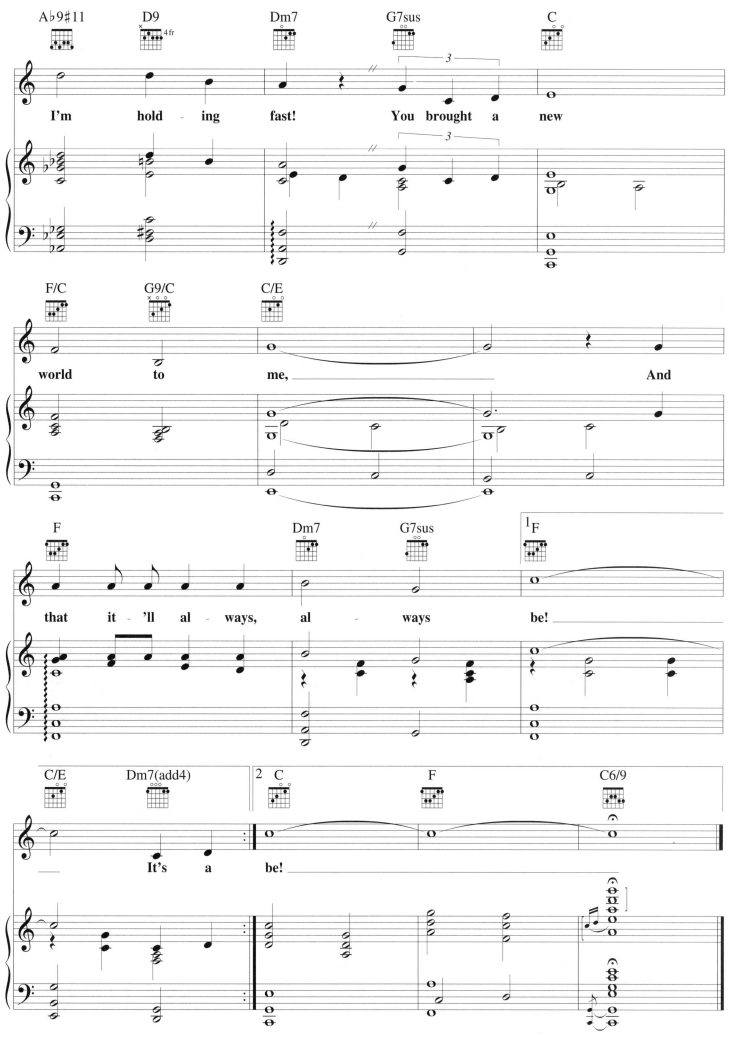

LA CANZONA DI DORETTA
(Chi Bel Sogno di Doretta)
featured in the Motion Picture A ROOM WITH A VIEW

Words and Music by
GIACOMO PUCCINI

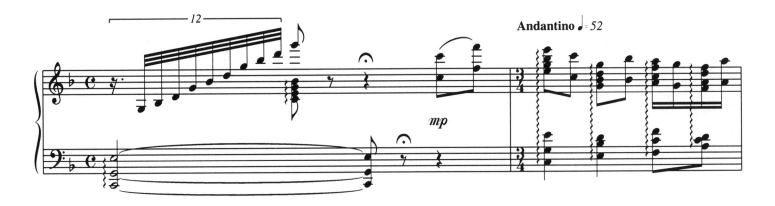

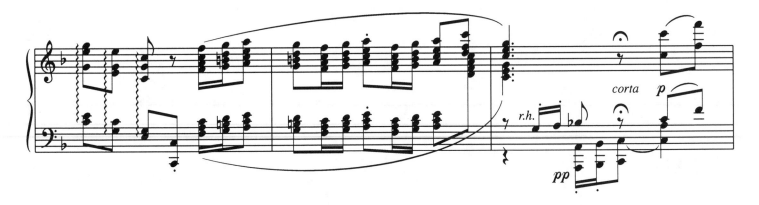

Sostenendo

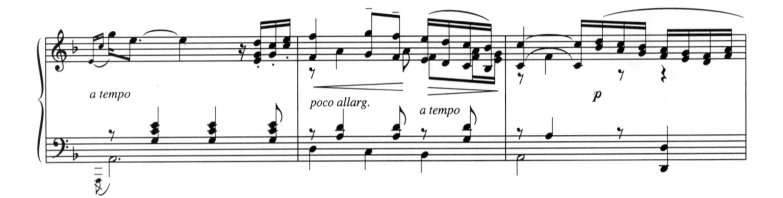

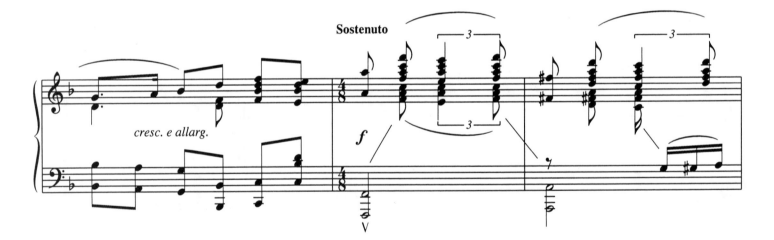

THE LAST TIME I FELT LIKE THIS
from SAME TIME, NEXT YEAR

Words by ALAN BERGMAN and MARILYN BERGMAN
Music by MARVIN HAMLISCH

LET'S FACE THE MUSIC AND DANCE

from the Motion Picture FOLLOW THE FLEET

Words and Music by
IRVING BERLIN

LONG AGO
(And Far Away)
from COVER GIRL

Words by IRA GERSHWIN
Music by JEROME KERN

Moderately

Drear - y days are o - ver; life's a four - leaf clo - ver.

Ses - sions of de - pres - sions are through. _____ Ev - 'ry

hope I longed for long a - go, comes true. _____

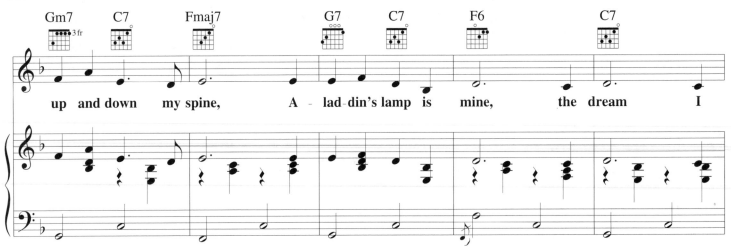

up and down my spine, A-lad-din's lamp is mine, the dream I

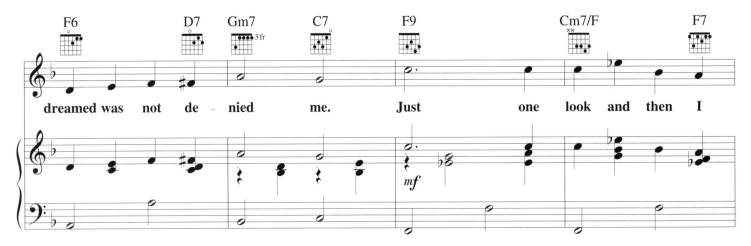

dreamed was not de-nied me. Just one look and then I

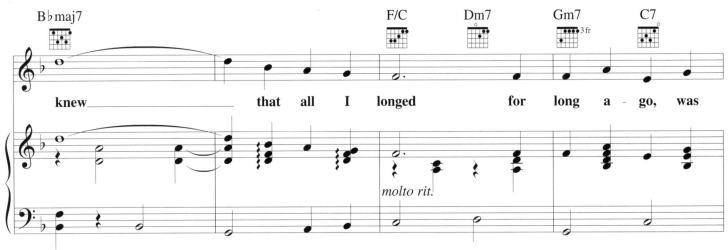

knew_____ that all I longed for long a-go, was

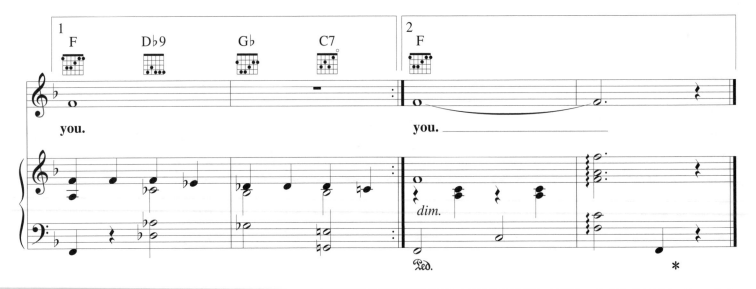

you. you._____

THE LOOK OF LOVE

from CASINO ROYALE

Words by HAL DAVID
Music by BURT BACHARACH

LOVE ME TENDER

from LOVE ME TENDER

Words and Music by ELVIS PRESLEY
and VERA MATSON

Moderately slow

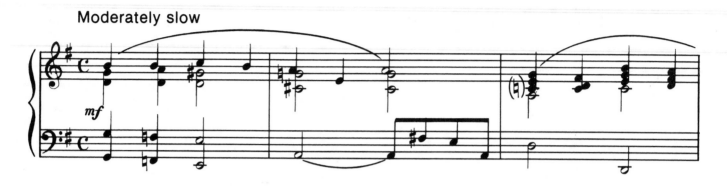

Verse

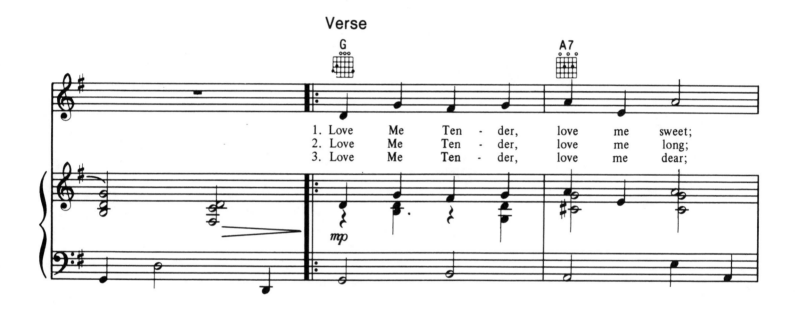

1. Love Me Ten - der, love me sweet;
2. Love Me Ten - der, love me long;
3. Love Me Ten - der, love me dear;

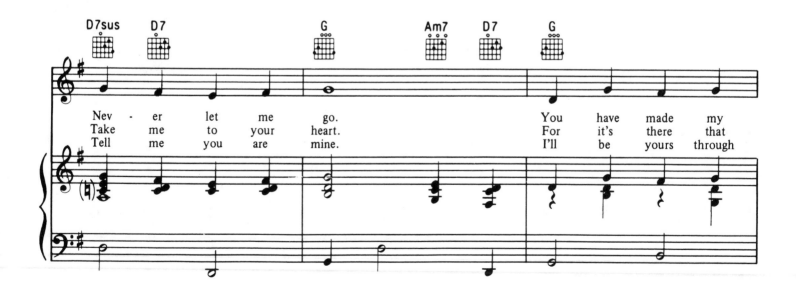

Nev - er let me go. You have made my
Take me to your heart. For it's there that
Tell me you are mine. I'll be yours through

EXTRA VERSE   4. When at last my dreams come true,
            Darling, this I know:
            Happiness will follow you
            Everywhere you go.

LOVE THEME FROM "THE EYES OF LAURA MARS"

(Prisoner)

from THE EYES OF LAURA MARS

Words and Music by KAREN LAWRENCE
and JOHN DESAUTELS

MONA LISA

featured in MONA LISA

Words and Music by JAY LIVINGSTON
and RAY EVANS

LOVE THEME FROM "ST. ELMO'S FIRE"

from the Motion Picture ST. ELMO'S FIRE

Words and Music by
DAVID FOSTER

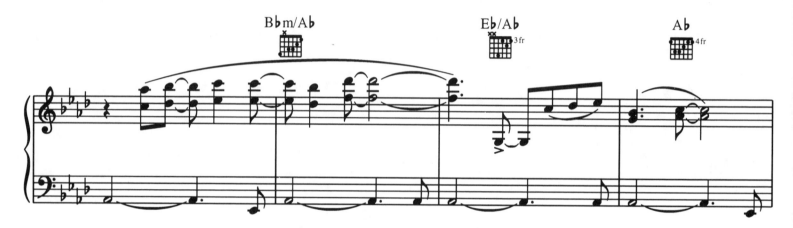

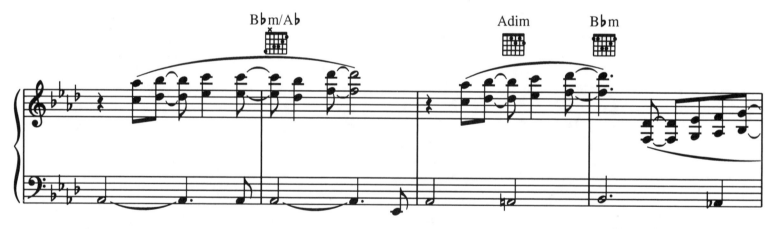

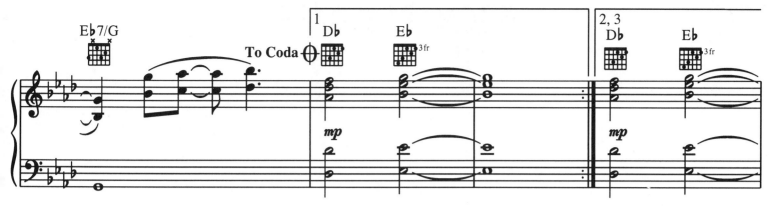

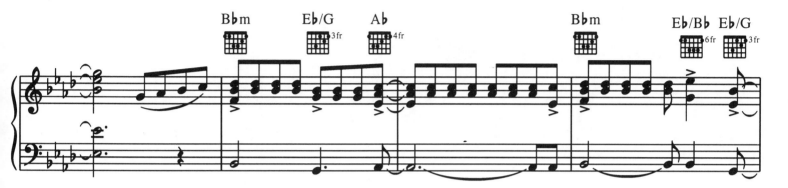

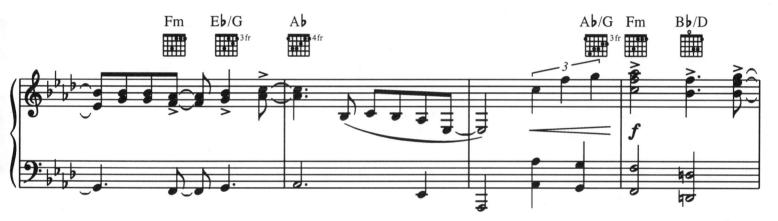

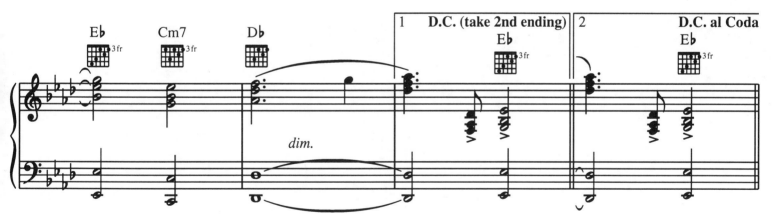

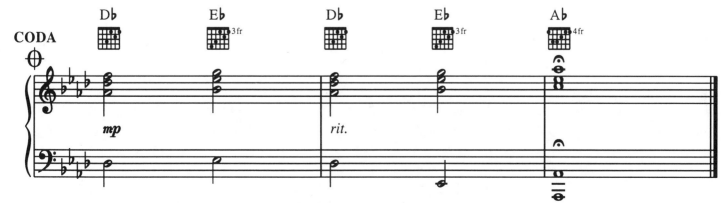

MOON RIVER
from the Paramount Picture BREAKFAST AT TIFFANY'S

Words by JOHNNY MERCER
Music by HENRY MANCINI

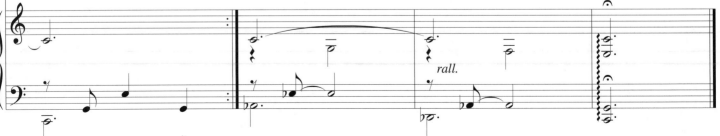

MORE
(Ti Guardero' Nel Cuore)
from the film MONDO CANE

Music by NINO OLIVIERO and RIZ ORTOLANI
Italian Lyrics by MARCELLO CIORCIOLINI
English Lyrics by NORMAN NEWELL

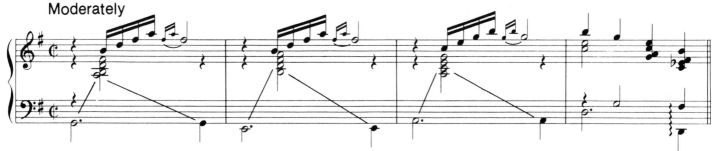

More than the great-est love the world has known;

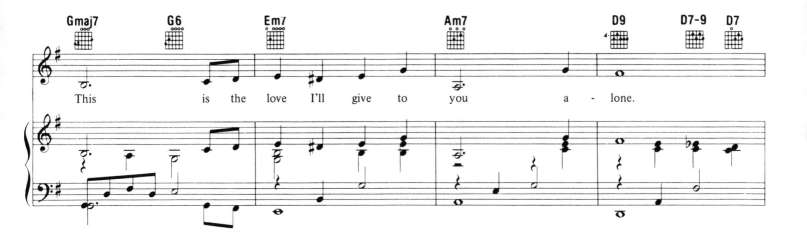

This is the love I'll give to you a - lone.

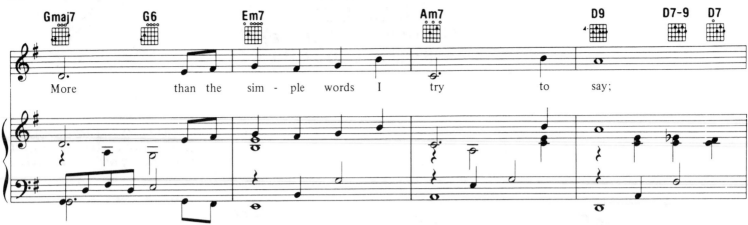

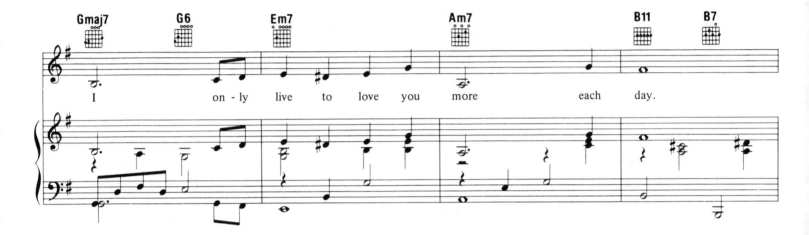

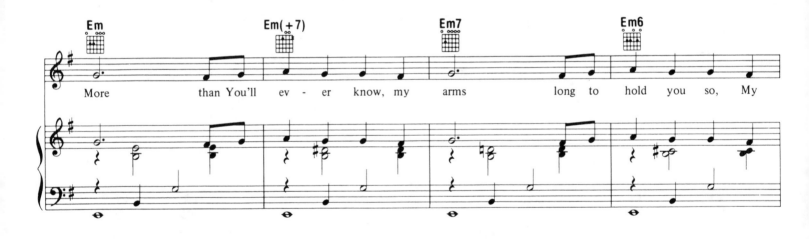

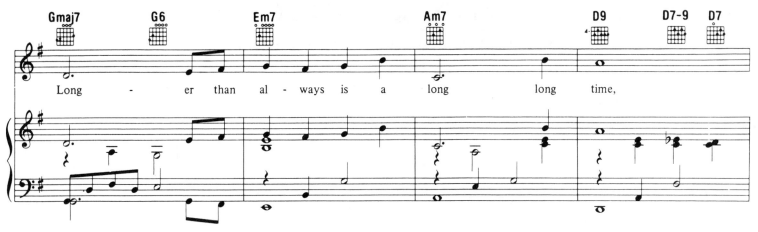

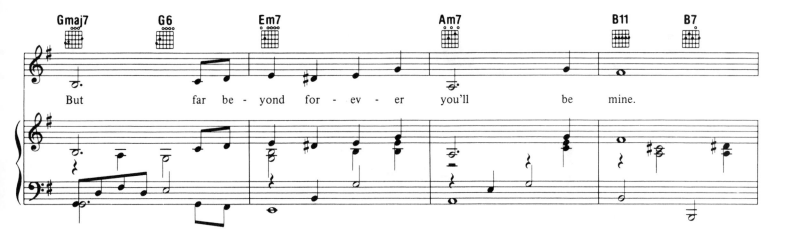

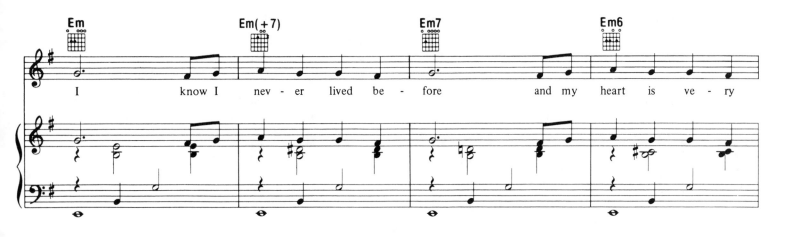

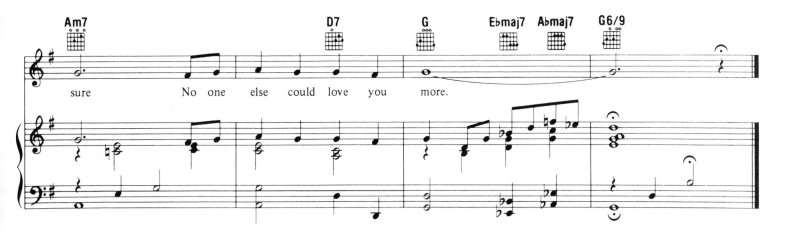

MOONLIGHT
from the Paramount Motion Picture SABRINA

Lyric by ALAN and MARILYN BERGMAN
Music by JOHN WILLIAMS

Moderate Bossa Nova

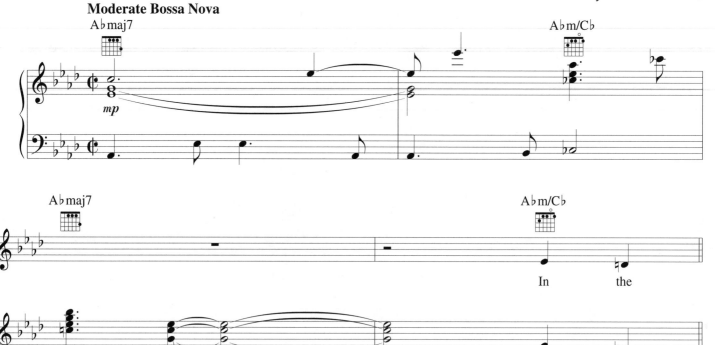

In the

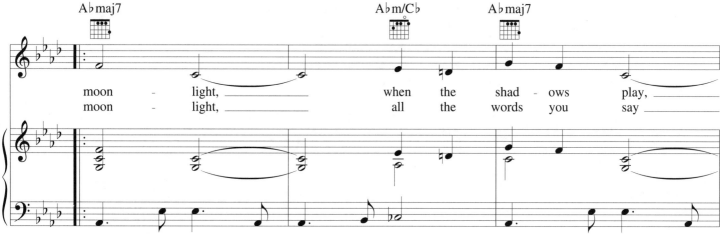

moon - light, _____ when the shad - ows play, _____
moon - light, _____ all the words you say _____

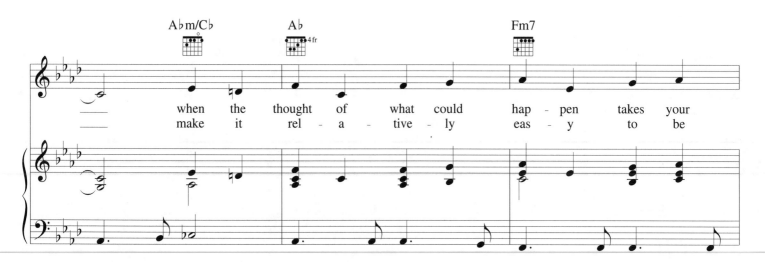

_____ when the thought of what could hap - pen takes your
_____ make it rel - a - tive - ly eas - y to be

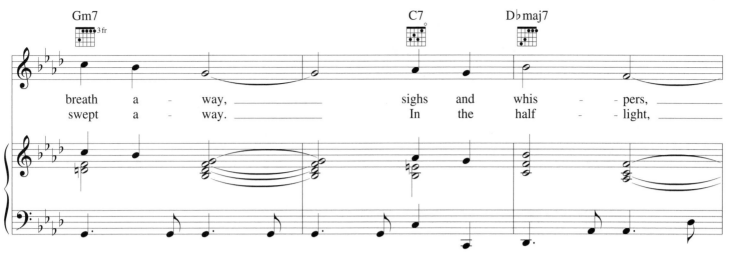

breath a - way, _____ sighs and whis - - pers,
swept a - way. _____ In the half - - light, _____

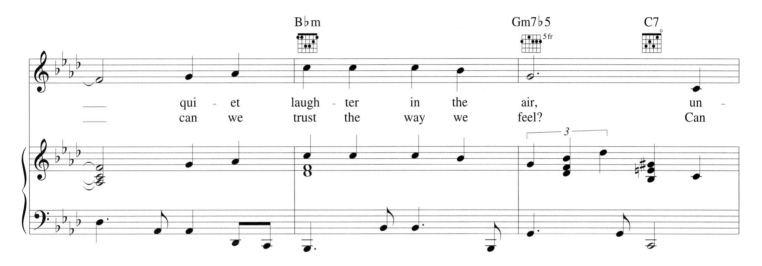

_____ qui - et laugh - ter in the air, _____ un -
can we trust the way we feel? Can

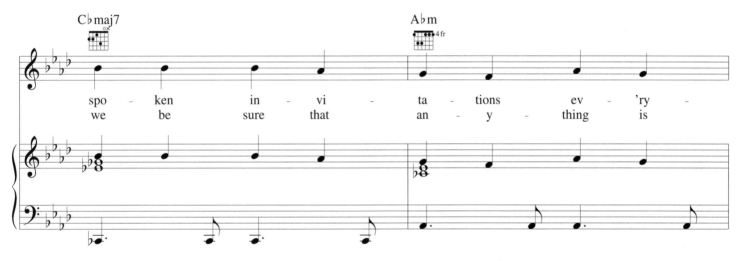

spo - ken in - vi - ta - tions ev - 'ry -
we be sure that an - y - thing is

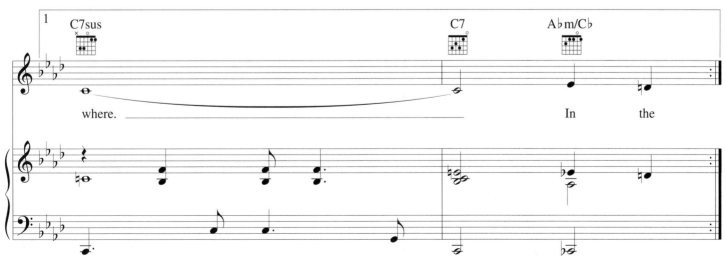

1

where. _____ In the

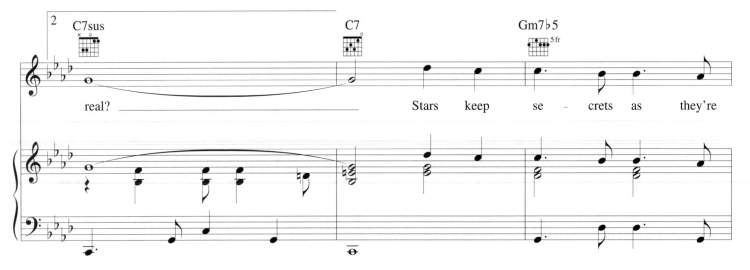

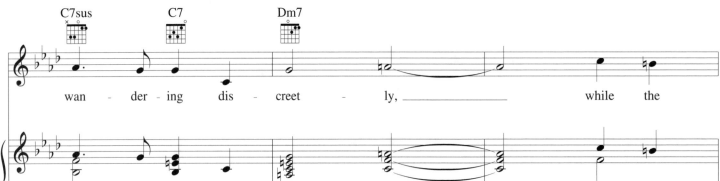

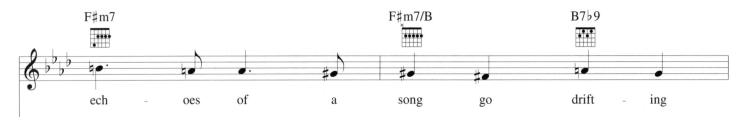

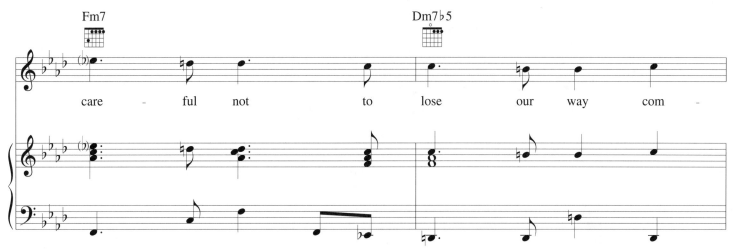

care - ful not to lose our way com -

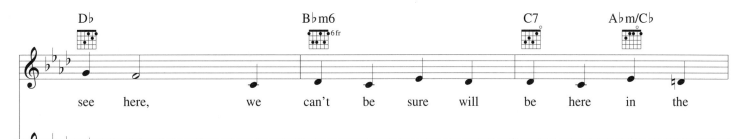

plete - ly, _____ or the mag - ic that we

see here, we can't be sure will be here in the

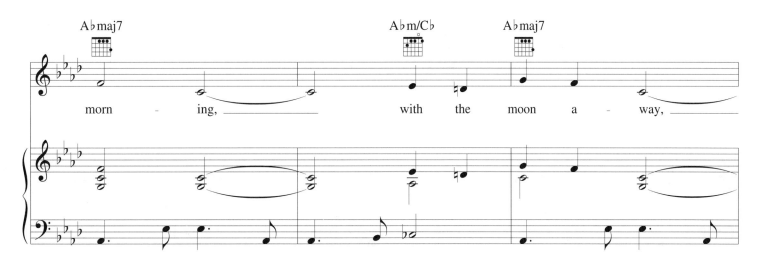

morn - ing, _____ with the moon a - way, _____

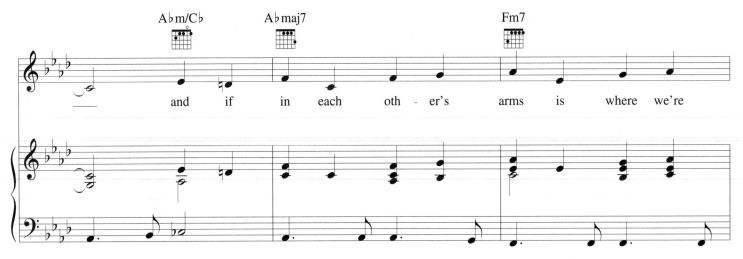

and if in each oth - er's arms is where we're

meant to stay, _____ in the love - light, _____

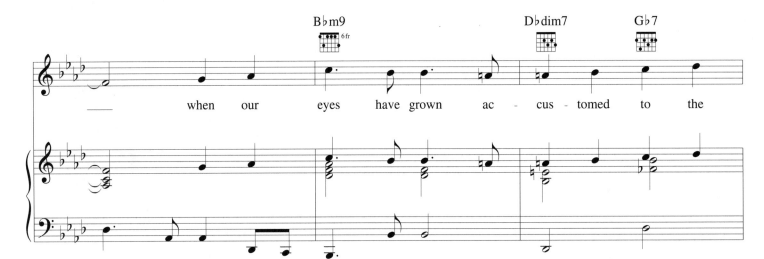

____ when our eyes have grown ac - cus - tomed to the

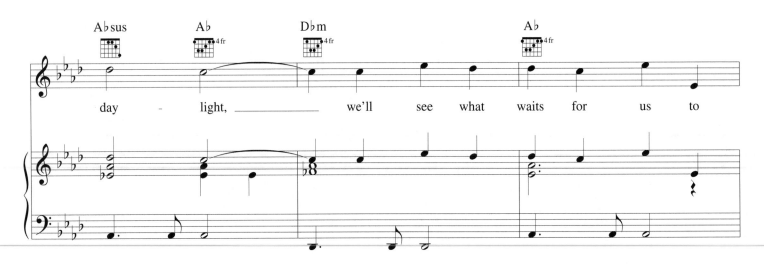

day - light, _____ we'll see what waits for us to

share; for all the things we've dreamed of in the

moon - light will be there. _____

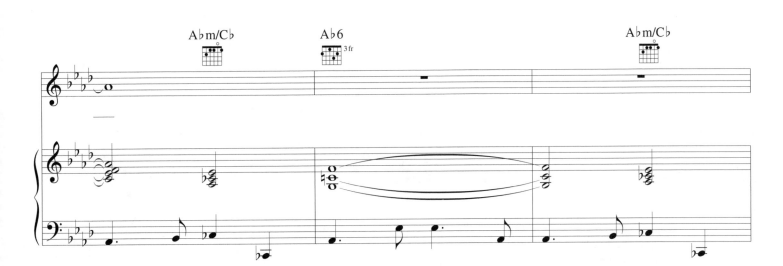

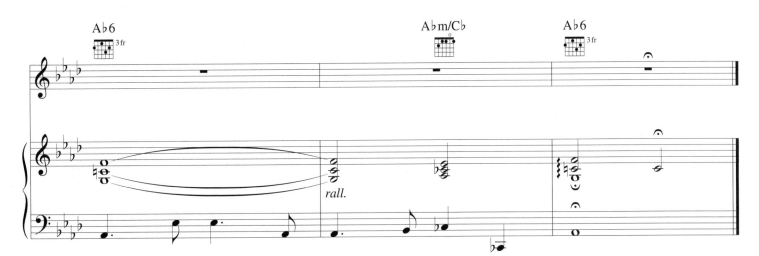

rall.

MOONLIGHT BECOMES YOU
from the Paramount Picture ROAD TO MOROCCO

Words by JOHNNY BURKE
Music by JAMES VAN HEUSEN

PICNIC
from the Columbia Technicolor Picture PICNIC

Words by STEVE ALLEN
Music by GEORGE W. DUNING

Dreamily

On a

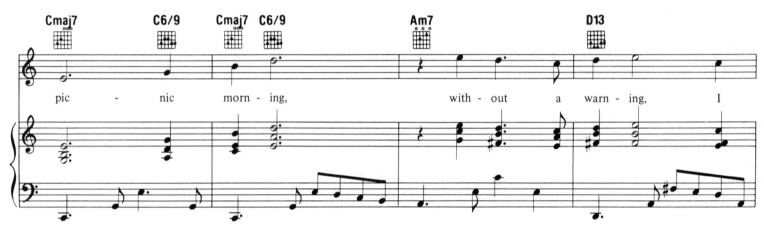

pic - nic morn - ing, with - out a warn - ing, I

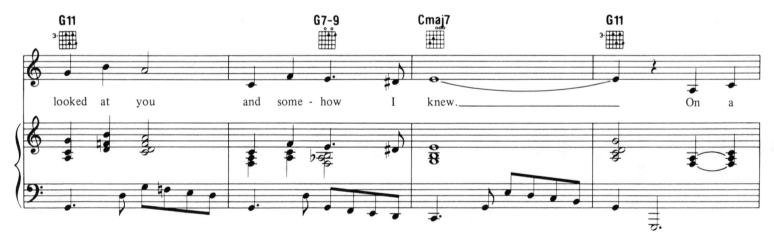

looked at you and some - how I knew. ____ On a

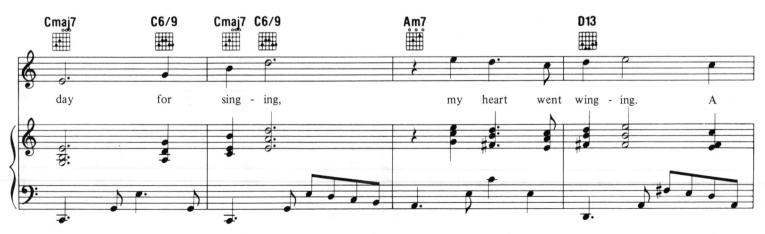

day for sing - ing, my heart went wing - ing. A

READY TO TAKE A CHANCE AGAIN
(Love Theme)
from the Paramount Picture FOUL PLAY

Words by NORMAN GIMBEL
Music by CHARLES FOX

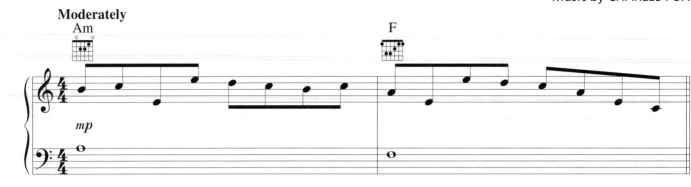

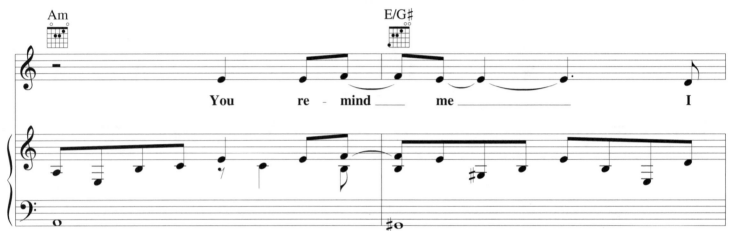

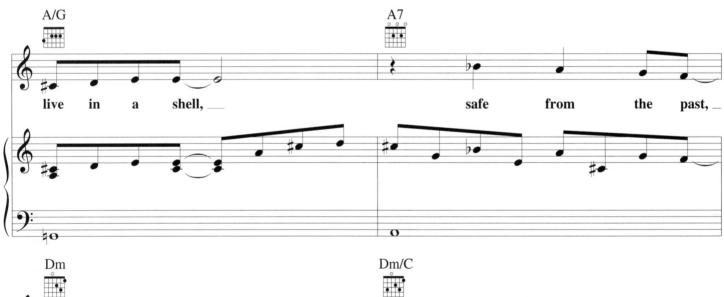

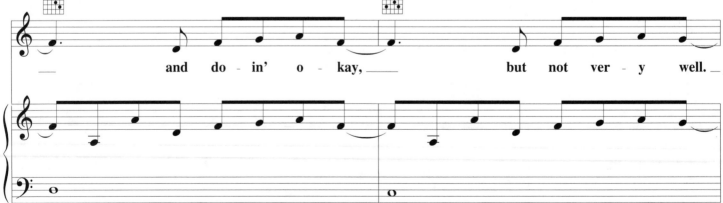

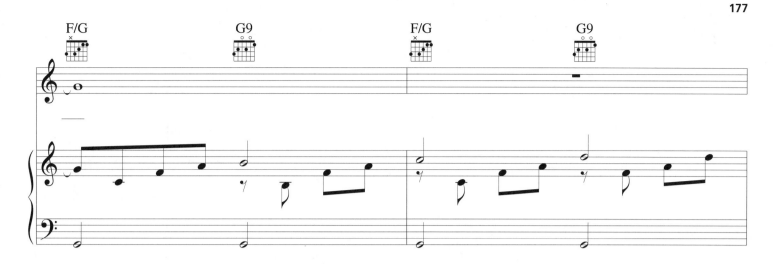

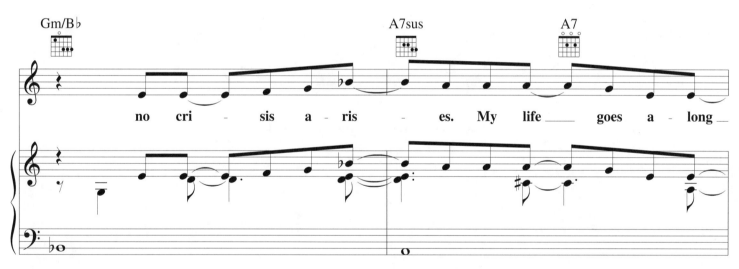

No jolts, __ no sur - pris - es,

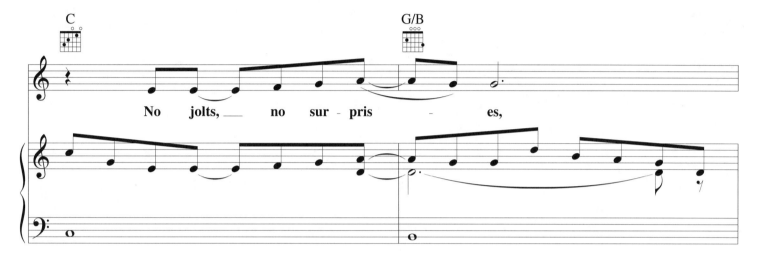

no cri - sis a - ris - es. My life __ goes a - long __

__ as it should, __ it's all ver - y nice, __ but

Repeat ad lib. and Fade

SOMETHING GOOD
from THE SOUND OF MUSIC

Lyrics and Music by
RICHARD RODGERS

Coda

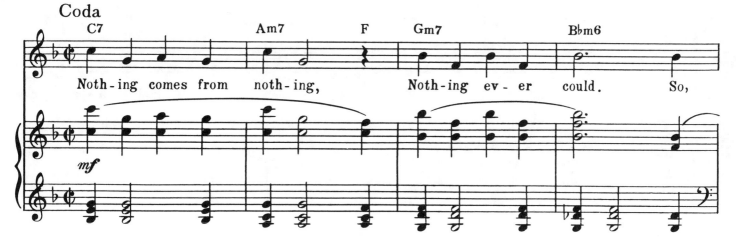

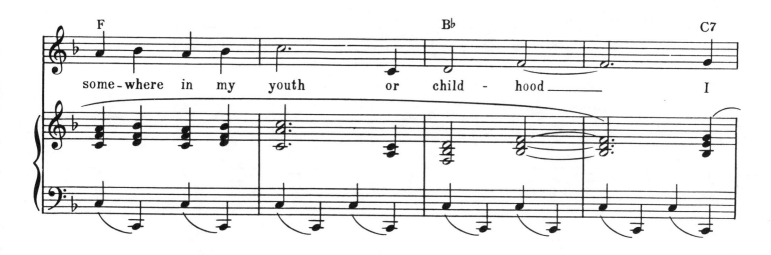

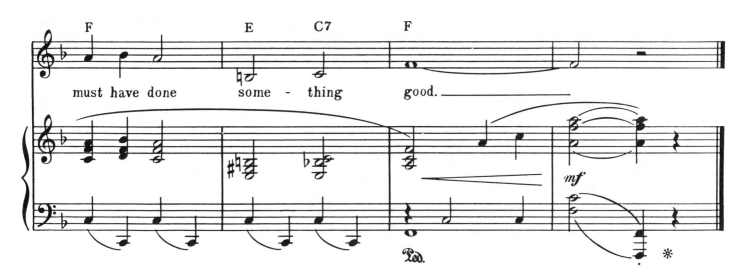

REMEMBER ME THIS WAY
from the Universal Motion Picture CASPER

Music by DAVID FOSTER
Lyrics by LINDA THOMPSON

MCA music publishing

stand-ing by ___ your side ___ in all ___ you ___ do. And I won't ev - er

leave, as long as you be - lieve. You just _____ be - lieve. ___

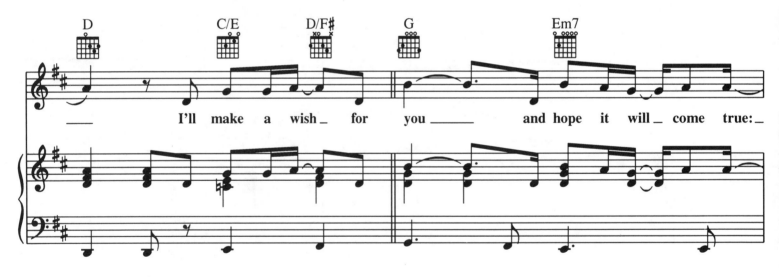

___ I'll make a wish ___ for you _____ and hope it will ___ come true: ___

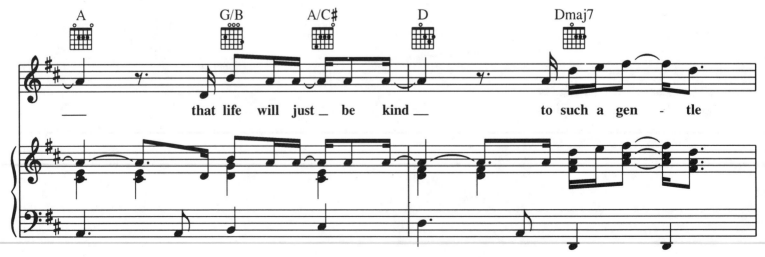

___ that life will just ___ be kind ___ to such a gen - tle

SEPARATE LIVES
Love Theme from WHITE NIGHTS

Words and Music by
STEPHEN BISHOP

SOMEWHERE, MY LOVE
Lara's Theme from DOCTOR ZHIVAGO

Lyric by PAUL FRANCIS WEBSTER
Music by MAURICE JARRE

SUMMERTIME IN VENICE
from the Motion Picture SUMMERTIME

English Words by CARL SIGMAN
Music by ICINI

THREE COINS IN THE FOUNTAIN

from THREE COINS IN THE FOUNTAIN

Words by SAMMY CAHN
Music by JULE STYNE

TENDERLY
from TORCH SONG

Lyric by JACK LAWRENCE
Music by WALTER GROSS

Moderately

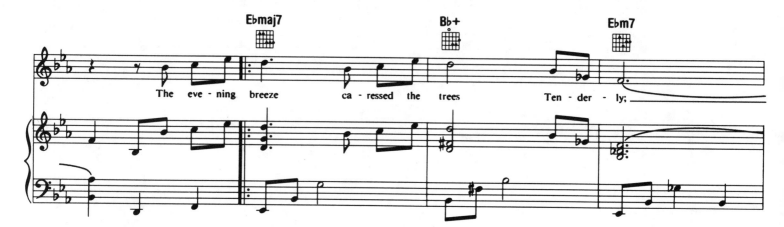

The eve-ning breeze ca-ressed the trees Ten-der-ly; The tremb-ling trees em-braced the breeze Ten-der-ly.

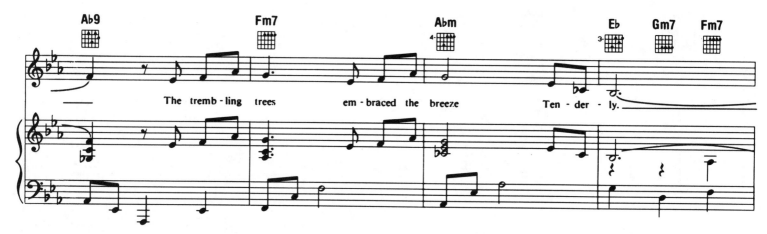

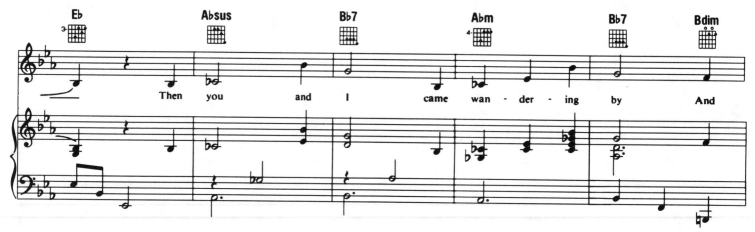

Then you and I came wan-der-ing by And

THANKS FOR THE MEMORY

from the Paramount Picture BIG BROADCAST OF 1938

Words and Music by LEO ROBIN
and RALPH RAINGER

THAT OLD BLACK MAGIC

from the Paramount Picture STAR SPANGLED RHYTHM

Words by JOHNNY MERCER
Music by HAROLD ARLEN

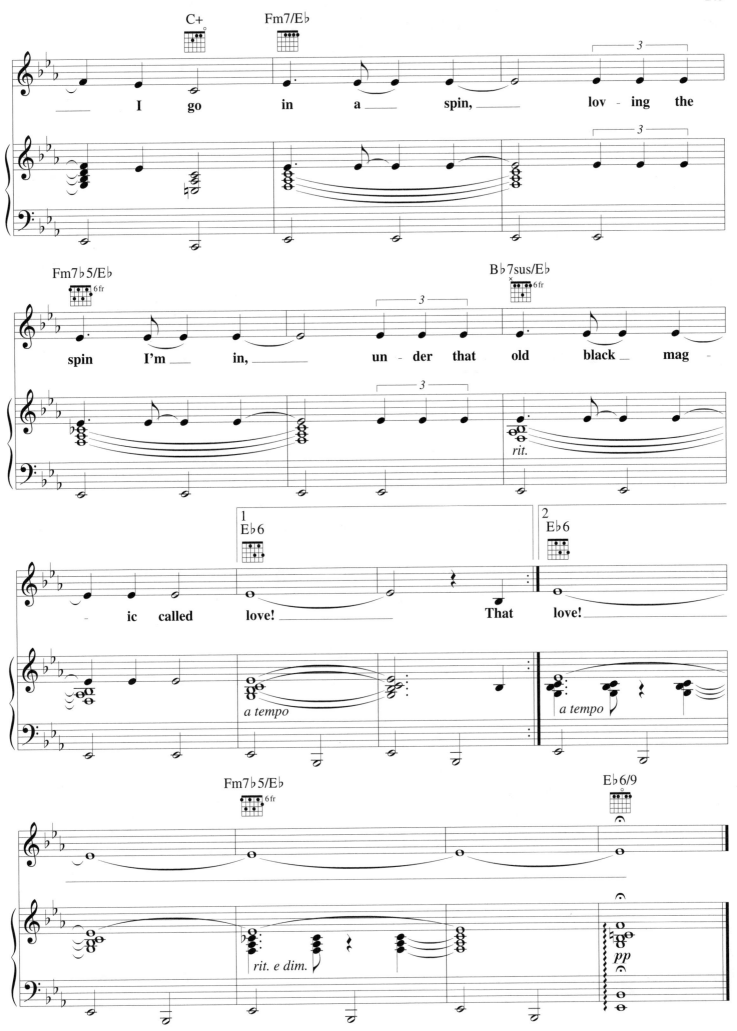

A TIME FOR US
(LOVE THEME)
from the Paramount Picture ROMEO AND JULIET

Words by LARRY KUSIK and EDDIE SNYDER
Music by NINO ROTA

Slowly and Expressively

thorns we will en-dure as we pass sure - ly through ev-'ry

storm. A time for us some-day there'll be _____ a

new world, _____ a world of shin-ing

hope for you and me. A time for me.

THE WAY YOU LOOK TONIGHT
from SWING TIME

Words by DOROTHY FIELDS
Music by JEROME KERN

TRUE LOVE
from HIGH SOCIETY

Words and Music by
COLE PORTER

Moderately Slow

I give to you and you give to me True Love, True Love. So, on and

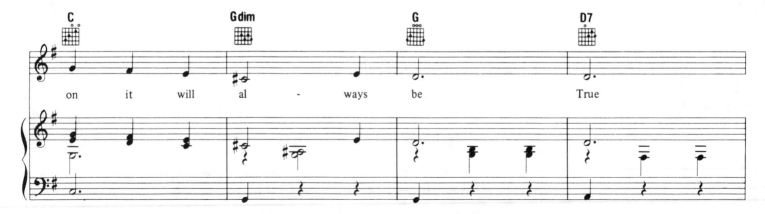

on it will al - ways be True

UNCHAINED MELODY
featured in the Motion Picture GHOST

Lyric by HY ZARET
Music by ALEX NORTH

Lone - ly riv - ers sigh,— "Wait for me,___ wait for me!"
All a - lone, I gaze___ at the stars,___ at the stars,

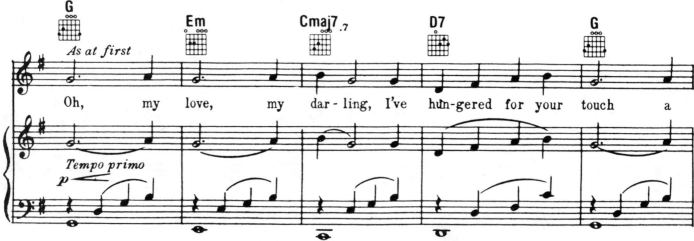

I'll be com - ing home,— wait for me! _____
Dream - ing of my love___ far a - way. _____

As at first

Oh, my love, my dar - ling, I've hun - gered for your touch a

Tempo primo
p

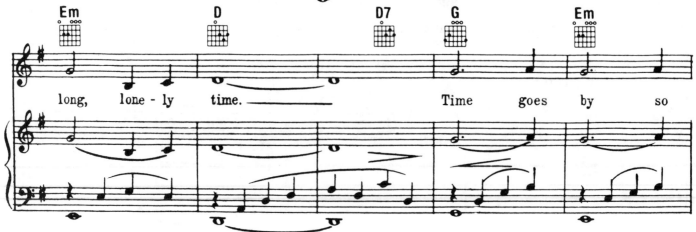

long, lone - ly time. _____ Time goes by so

UP WHERE WE BELONG

from the Paramount Picture AN OFFICER AND A GENTLEMAN

Words by WILL JENNINGS
Music by BUFFY SAINTE-MARIE and JACK NITZSCHE

Soulfully

Who knows what to- mor-row brings; ___ in a
Some hang on to "used to be," ___ live their

world, few hearts sur- vive? All I know is the
lives look- ing be- hind. All we have is

way I feel; ___ when it's real, I keep it a- live. ___
here and now; ___ all our life, out there to find. ___

The

Love lift us up where we be-long, _____ where the

ea - gles cry, _____ on a moun - tain high. _____

Love lift us up where we be-long _____ far from the

Repeat ad lib. and Fade

world we know; _____ where the clear winds blow. _____

WHEN I FALL IN LOVE

featured in the TriStar Motion Picture SLEEPLESS IN SEATTLE

Words by EDWARD HEYMAN
Music by VICTOR YOUNG

WHERE IS YOUR HEART
(The Song from Moulin Rouge)
from MOULIN ROUGE

Music by GEORGE AURIC

WHERE DO I BEGIN
(Love Theme)
from the Paramount Picture LOVE STORY

Words by CARL SIGMAN
Music by FRANCIS LAI

Where do I be-gin _____ to tell the sto-ry of how
With her first hel-lo _____ she gave a mean-ing to this

great a love can be, _____ the sweet love sto-ry that is
emp-ty world of mine. _____ There'd nev-er be an-oth-er

old-er than the sea, the sim-ple truth a-bout the
love, an-oth-er time; she came in-to my life and

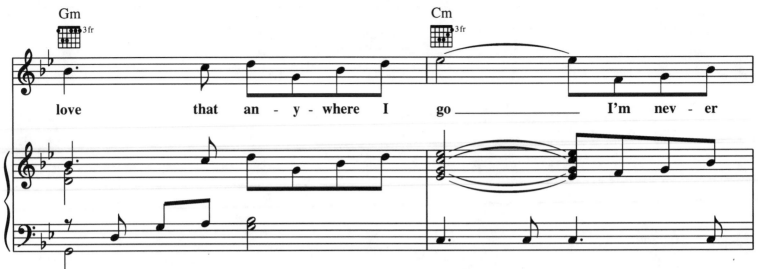

love that an - y - where I go _____ I'm nev - er

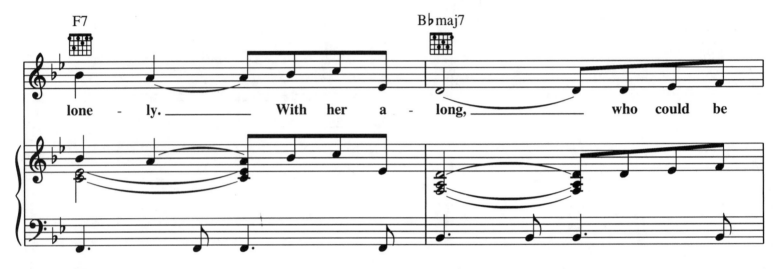

lone - ly. _____ With her a - long, _____ who could be

lone - ly? _____ I reach for her hand, _____ it's al - ways there. _____

How long does it last? _____ Can love be meas - ured by the

YOU'RE NEARER
from TOO MANY GIRLS

Words by LORENZ HART
Music by RICHARD RODGERS

Moderately

Time is a heal-er, but it can-not heal my heart,_____ My

mind says I've for-got-ten you and then I feel my heart, The

miles lie be-tween us, but your fin-gers touch my own,_____ You're

YOU MUST LOVE ME
from the Cinergi Motion Picture EVITA

Words by TIM RICE
Music by ANDREW LLOYD WEBBER

Flowing ♩=92

1. Where do we go from here?
2. (See additional lyrics)

This is-n't where we in-tend-ed to be. ___ We had it all, ___ you be-

lieved ___ in me, ___ I be-lieved ___ in you. ___

feel - ing   fright - ened you'll slip   a - way,   you must love

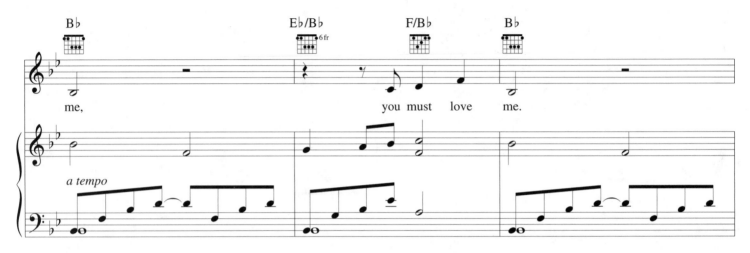

me,   you must love me.

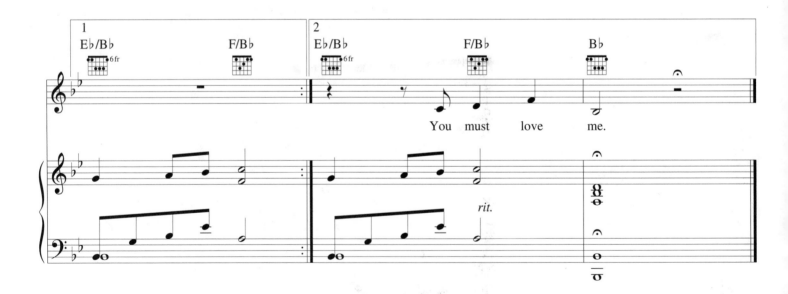

You must love me.

Additional Lyrics

Verse 2: *(Instrumental 8 bars)*
Why are you at my side?
How can I be any use to you now?
Give me a chance and I'll let you see how
Nothing has changed.
Deep in my heart I'm concealing
Things that I'm longing to say,
Scared to confess what I'm feeling
Frightened you'll slip away,
You must love me.